Amiga A1200

Next Steps

Bruce Smith Books

Amiga A1200
Next Steps

Learn how to get the very most from your Amiga A1200

Peter Fitzpatrick

Bruce Smith Books

© Peter Fitzpatrick 1993
ISBN: 1-873308-24-8
First Edition: November 1993

Editors: Mark Webb, Bruce Smith
Typesetting: Bruce Smith Books Ltd

Bruce Smith Books is an imprint of Bruce Smith Books Limited.

Published by: Bruce Smith Books Limited. PO Box 382, St. Albans, Herts, AL2 3JD. Telephone: (0923) 894355 – Fax: (0923) 894366.

Registered in England No. 2695164.

Registered Office: Worplesdon Chase, Worplesdon, Guildford, Surrey, GU3 3LA

Printed and bound in the UK by Ashford Colour Press, Gosport.

The Author

PETER FITZPATRICK was thrown in at the computing deep end when he woke up one day and found himself as Deputy Editor of *A&B Computing* magazine – a publication devoted to Acorn computers. Not knowing anything about the subject he decided it might be wise to learn...

Since then he went on to become editor of *A&B Computing* and launched its successor *Archimedes World*. His experience of the Amiga has been brief but brutal – an A500 quickly followed by an A1200 with several Bruce Smith books devoured in the process.

He lives in historic St Albans and dreams of finishing his best-selling travel book. One day, maybe, one day.

Contents

Preface **15**

1 Workbench **17**
Workbench Menu 18
Window Menu 20
Icons Menu 22
Tool Menu 26
Short-cuts..26

2 Extras! Extras! **29**
Preferences...30
Tools Drawer 36
Commodities...38

3 AmigaDOS **43**
Getting Going 39
Filing Cabinets...44
Writing Scripts 48
Miscellany 50
Wildcards etc 53

4 MultiView **55**
It Doesn't Work..56
On the Menu 57
Hyperactivity 57
Dungeon Text..58
Other Uses..61
AmigaDOS 3 61
The Dungeon...62

5 Totally RAD **67**
Hard and Fast 68
RAD Diskcopy...71

6   The Printed Word 73

Home Publishing 74
Type and Fonts 74
Bitmap or Outline....................................75
Choosing Fonts 76
Intellifont 76
Installing Outlines 76
Modifying Outlines..................................77
Variable Change 78

7   The Protection Racket 81

Fly the Flags!...82
More Flags 83
Workbench Flags 85
Archiving...88
Bit of a Squash 88

8   All is Not Lost.....................91

No, Not Me...92
Rescue Stations 93
File Paranoia..93
Disk Storage..94

9   Start from Scratch 97

Startup Sequence 98
Fine Tuning..102
Boot Disks..102

10   MORE AmigaDOS...................105

And There's More 105
PCD...107
Path to Success 108
MEmacs 108
Search me, Guv.......................................109
Sort Of..110
Join the Club...111
Flexible Programs...................................111
IF...ELSE 111
Choice Request 112

INSTALL 113
ADDBUFFERS 114
MOUNT 114

11 One Liners 117

Cracking the Shell 117
File Displays...118
Making Dates 118
On the List 119
Making Notes..120
Forced Eviction 120
More Protections 121
INFO...122
MAKEDIR...122
Speed Reading 122
STATUS...123
Copy Cats 123
Launching Apps..124

12 Print Out 125

Unpacking...126
Choosing a Driver...127
Printer Bugs 128
Printing Text Files 128
Printing Graphics 129
Trouble-shooting 131
Driver Workings 132
Change Device 133
Experiment! 134

13 Growing Pains..............137

Extra Disk Drive 138
Rapid Expansion 139
FPUs and Co-pros...140
Joysticks...140
Printers...140
Modems..141
Fax Machines..142
CD-ROM...142
CD32 143

Scanners...144
Machine Chatter....................................144
One Step Further....................................146

14 Put It On Display.................149

How it all Works....................................150
Multi-syncs..150
Monitor Types.......................................150
Display Modes.......................................152
Mode Properties....................................152
IControl..155
More Colours...156
Catch 22..156
Lost Memory...157
Interlacing...157
Graphics Cards.....................................157
Mode Properties....................................158

15 Not So Hard After All.........159

Hard Drive Facts...................................159
No IDEa?...150
How it Works...160
Which Hard Disk...................................161
Up and Running....................................161
Option Two..162
Disclaimer...162
Fitting the Drive....................................163
Partioning..166
HDToolbox...166
Loading WB3...167
Almost There...168

16 A Hard Act to Follow.........171

Loading Up..172
Floppy Boots...172
Hard Games..173
Utility Help...173
Beware of..174
No Parking...176
Backing Up..176

Other Possibilities 177
Hard Disk Set-ups 178
Problem Solving 178
Up and Running 180

17 Improve Your Memory........183
How to Fit Them 184
PCMCIA..184
Memory Cards 185
The Down Side 186
Other Uses...186
Just a Wee Dram..188
PrepCard 189
A Hard Choice..190

18 Moving Pictures.......................191
Graphics Images..192
Animation 192
From Television..193
Digitising..193
Camcorders..194
LookOut, Disney!...196
Sounds Good 197
Graphics Cards 197

19 Sounds Good...............................199
Sampling...200
Trackers 201
Writing Music...201
Progressing 202
Singing 204
File Formats..204

20 Playing Silly Games.................207
All Work, No Play 207
Joystick Wagglers 208
Adventures 209
Flight Sims..210
Puzzles 211

Strategy 211
Game Over 212
Hints and Tips 212
Hardware 213

21 Mind Your Language 215

Long Ago 215
Hard and Soft 216
Engine Room 217
Language Types 218
Portability 218
Why Languages 219
Command Syntax 220
Same Routine 220
Program Writing..221
ARexx 221
AmigaDOS 222
AMOS 222
All at C 224
Amiga BASIC 224

22 Take Good Care Of... 225

Floppy Disks 225
Monitors...226
Mice..226
Coffee & Smoke...227
Hard Disks 227
Guru Meditations 228
Software Crashes..228
Viruses..228
How they Work..229
Virus Spotting..230
Take Precautions! 230
Antibiotics..231

A The Disk 233

B Amiga Guides 235

Insider Guides

#1:	Updating a window	23
#2:	Tidying up with hot keys	27
#3:	Sound Preferences	31
#4:	Background pictures	37
#5:	Function key shortcuts	41
#6:	Writing a script in Ed	49
#7:	Editing a picture	63
#8:	Mounting a RAD Disk	71
#9:	Bitmap and outline fonts	75
#10:	Creating a bitmap font	79
#11:	Protecting a file from deletion	87
#12:	Rescuing a file using ARestaure	95
#13:	Using REQUESTCHOICE	113
#14:	ReadMe files with MORE – Part 1	115
#15:	ReadMe files with MORE – Part 2	116
#16:	Using LIST to create files	121
#17:	Crossing between DOSs	147
#18:	Choosing display modes	151
#19:	Getting software to run from a hard disk	175
#20:	The Workbench partition	179
#21:	Backing up with ABackup	181
#22:	Video hardware combinations	198
#23:	Getting started with OctaMED	203
#24:	Running early games	213
#25:	Starting in ARexx	223
#26:	Avoiding the virus menace	229

Get the most from your A1200.

Learn how to ...

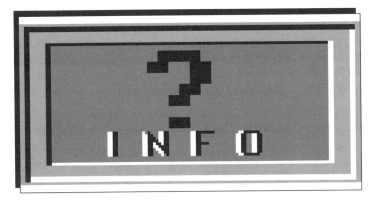

Y ou're an Amiga A1200 owner. You've mastered the basics of operating the machine and now you want to find out more about what you can do with the machine.

Read on. This book takes the exploration of the A1200 one stage further and provides a grounding in many of the areas open to A1200 owners: making music, printing documents, creating graphics, video editing and even takes a look at programming.

The book also aims to speed up your computing. That's not just a question of making the A1200 itself go physically faster, although that is one of the options, but extra memory or buying a hard disk drive or a second floppy disk drive will make *you* work faster. So will an understanding of the language that is at the heart of the A1200 – AmigaDOS. All these subjects are covererd in *Next Steps*.

Owning a computer can rapidly turn into an expensive business and I've discussed the things you should consider before parting with your money. I can't tell you which of the many options is best for your own particular needs but what I can do is provide the information for you to make your own decisions.

There are many add-ons to the A1200 that you will want to consider as you get more ambitious: more memory, another disk drive, better monitors, accelerators cards, modems and so on all of which are covered. I've even included a brief section on games because if you're not playing them then you're not getting the most from your A1200 – and getting the most from your A1200 is the whole purpose of this book.

There are two chapters on choosing and fitting a hard disk drive. I've provided a step-by-step guide to installing a hard disk drive yourself and then formatting it, partitioning it and setting it up as a boot disk. And if you didn't understand the jargon used in that last sentence you needn't worry either – that gets explained as well.

The one thing I can't promise, though, is to turn you into an Amiga expert. I'm not sure when that exalted state arrives but it takes more than reading one book. There are plenty more volumes where this one came from. Appendix B at the end of the book provides details on AmigaDOS, AMOS, ARrexx, C and Assembler programming, Printers and Amiga Games.

There is a *Next Steps* disk of freely distributable software to accompany the chapters in this book. It includes some of the most commonly sought after utilities to make the whole computing process that much easier. Details can be found in Appendix B.

If you find that this book assumes too much knowledge then don't despair! The Insider Guide to the Amiga A1200 should get you on the right tracks soon enough.

The emphasis is on practical examples with step-by-step Insider Guides to take you by the hand and lead you safely through the minefield. Happy computing.

1

The Workbench is the starting point for all life on the Amiga. Get to grips with it and you're well on the way to success with your A1200...

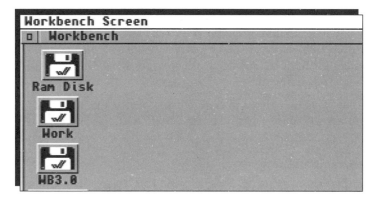

*T*he starting place for most A1200 use is via the Workbench. That's the blue and grey screen that greets you on booting up. Using the *WIMP* system of windows, icons, mouse and pointer you are presented with a pictorial representation of the various files and disks that are available to you. It has been designed to be as easy and intuitive to use as the designers could make it. Thus disks are represented by little pictures (icons) of disks and directories are represented by drawers (they can also be called "drawers" if you prefer). Opening a drawer requires a double-click and then its contents are revealed.

It is as well to get as familiar as possible with the workings of this system as it is fundamental to the Amiga's everyday use. However, as there are so many options available to the user a little confusion can be excused. This chapter provides an explanation of all the Workbench menu options and how they can be used.

Workbench Menu

The Workbench menu contains seven options all of which offer actions that are broadly applicable to the Workbench screen as a whole. Each of these are summarised below.

Backdrop

This one is largely a matter of aesthetic preference. Do you want your Workbench screen to be inside a pretty, blue-framed window? From a purist's point of view the answer should be "yes". Workbench is a program like any other multi-tasking program you can run on the A1200. With the exception of certain tasks that run completely in the background they all operate from within a window so why should Workbench be any different?

The alternative view is that the blue border itself takes up a finite amount of screen space which can be better used elsewhere. You choose.

Execute Command...

Selecting this option pops up a request window headed "Execute a File". This can be used as a convenient way of entering one-line commands that would normally be entered through the Shell. For example try typing in VERSION and either clicking on OK or hitting the <Return> key. The VERSION command is rather superfluous in the normal run of things but it does demonstrate how this option works. In this case another window is produced, the Output window, which tells us that the A1200 is using Kickstart version number 39.106 and Workbench number 39.29. The numbers on your machine may differ to mine but then my A1200 is probably older than yours! This option is the subject of the "One Liners" chapter.

Redraw All

It is possible that a software glitch can cause problems with the screen display causing parts of the screen to become blanked off for example. Redraw All should solve this problem.

Update All

Certain changes that are made to the items on screen are not made immediately apparent. As an example, open the Ram Disk window and then try entering the following command via the Execute Command option:

COPY DF0:WBSTARTUP.INFO TO RAM:

What this does is copy the .info file from the Workbench disk across to the Ram Disk. So why can't we see it? For the Workbench to keep constantly updating all the windows would waste the power of the machine so, for convenience's sake (its convenience that is, not yours) it doesn't bother. Generally this isn't a problem – after all you're normally the one who's instigated any changes so you should know about them. Using the Update option redisplays the window and will miraculously make the "WBStartup" icon appear.

Last Message

Try this for size. Take your Workbench disk out of the drive. Now double-click on its icon. What happens? What should happen is a Requester window opens saying "Please insert volume Workbench3.0 in any drive" with two buttons marked "Retry" or "Cancel". Click on Retry and the Workbench program will try to read a disk that isn't there and the same requester will be displayed again. Press "Cancel" and Workbench will accept that you are no longer interested in looking at the contents of that particular disk and let you get on with something else. The third option available here is to put the disk back in the drive. This time, before you've even had a chance to click on "Retry" the A1200 has started doing it for you and opens the disk's window. For this example though we'll choose the "Cancel" option and put the disk back in its drive. Across the top of the white bar is written the message "This drawer cannot be opened". It explains why your disk reading attempt failed. Periodically the Workbench program will flash all manner of messages to you and one way of keeping track of them is to use the Last Message option. All it does is repeat the previous information.

About...

Another option which doesn't hold any great fascination, solely providing the same information as the VERSION command. This information can be useful when trying to get certain bits of software to run. As newer versions of both Kickstart and Workbench are produced they can incorporate features not available to earlier models. Some items of software will exploit this advantage and will usually have information somewhere on them saying "Requires Kickstart version 39.1 and Workbench version 39.2" or some such.

In practice this isn't going to happen too often for two reasons. The first is that minor version changes rarely make a big difference to the way most software runs. The second reason is that most software manufacturers will try and make their software run on as many machines as possible; that way they can sell more copies!

Quit...

Like any other program Workbench offers the chance to Quit. Try using this option and a request window will double-check that this is what you want to do. You can choose to Quit but you're not left with a lot once you have.

A small confession here. When I tried using this option, in writing this chapter, Workbench wouldn't let me quit. Instead it informed me that it "Cannot Quit yet, there are 1 WB launched program(s)"

The launched Workbench program in question was the ClickToFront commodity which I have kept in the WBStartup directory. Whenever Workbench is loaded this program is automatically loaded too. This failsafe mechanism prevents you from quitting Workbench while any program that relies on it is in operation. Not desperately important if you're only using "ClickToFront" but invaluable if you're in the middle of wordprocessing and haven't saved your work.

Window Menu

As you might expect these options are only applicable to the currently selected window. Double-click on the Ram Disk icon and a display window opens. Now click outside that window in the Workbench window. Notice how the borders of the windows change colour. Whichever one has been clicked in most recently is the "currently selected" one and is identified by its blue border. Try looking at the Window menu options when first the Workbench window and, secondly, the Ram Disk display window are currently selected. When the Ram Disk display window is selected all the options appear in bold black type. Not only that but when the pointer is moved over the options, those that can be selected are illuminated as white on black rather than just remaining fuzzy and grey.

What is happening is the Workbench program decides which of the options are feasible to perform on the window you have selected. If it's not possible – you can't choose it.

New Drawer

The New Drawer option creates a new drawer – that's a directory with a .info file. It places a drawer in your chosen window and brings up a requester window so that you can rename these directories should you be unhappy with "Unnamed1", "Unnamed2" and so on. As it has a .info file a directory icon is displayed.

Open Parent

Double-clicking on a directory icon displays its contents. If it has sub-directories then you can open as many of these the same way and so on down and down the directory branches. Pretty soon the screen becomes covered with opened windows and trying to find your way around gets hectic. Close any unwanted windows and leave just those you absolutely need. To step back up the directory tree from any given directory just use the "Open Parent" option.

Close

Close closes the currently selected window. It's only real use is going to be when the close gadget is obscured from view by a multitude of other windows.

Update

Like the Update All option in the Workbench menu, except that this one just concentrates on the currently selected window. It is therefore, quicker.

Select Contents

Click in a directory window to designate it as the currently selected one and then click on this option. The icons are now in their *reversed out* format signifying they have all been selected. If you want to try and drag all the selected icons, say to another directory, then press the Shift button first.

Clean Up

When you drag files from one directory to another they tend to end up plonked one on top of another. Try creating a new directory on the Ram Disk and then dragging some Workbench icons to it. They tend to sit wherever they have been left, usually obscuring anything beneath. The "Clean Up" option solves this problem by reorganising the window items around each other.

Snapshot

The previous example was all well and good but if you now close the directory window and re-open it, what happens? The window is presented in its pre-cleaned up style. "Clean Up" the window once more and move any icons round to your own taste. Once you're happy select the "Snapshot >> All" option and a record will be stored of where all the icons sit when the window is opened.

The "Snapshot >> Window" option dictates where the window will be opened and what size and shape it assumes. So if, for example, you want the Ram Disk window to appear at the bottom right of the Workbench window when you open it then move it there and select the "Snapshot >> Window" option.

Show

In day-to-day use Workbench keeps a large number of files hidden from view. For a file to appear on-screen it needs to have a .info file associated with it. Most of the time this is perfectly acceptable as it reduces the amount of clutter around the place but if you want to see what commands are available in the C: directory for example it's not a whole lot of use. The "Show >> All Files" option does just that on the window in question. "Show >> Only Icons" reverts to the default setting.

View By

The final option on this menu lets you choose how the files within the window are displayed. The "View By >> Icon" option is the default setting. The other three display files without their associated icons. All you get is the name of each file, a written description of its type – eg Drawer – and information about the last time it was saved and its flags; similar in fact to when you use the LIST command in AmigaDOS. While this form of display may not be as attractive as the icon-based option it does have one enormous advantage and that's size – they take up a lot less room this way. The three remaining options let you view files by Name (in alphabetical order), Date (most recent first) and Size (smallest first).

Icons Menu

The opposite of the Windows menu as all the operations you can perform here have to be done to one or more icons.

Open

Click once on the Ram Disk icon. Its reversed out look signifies that it has been selected. To open the Ram Disk window select the "Open"

Insider Guide #1: Updating a window.

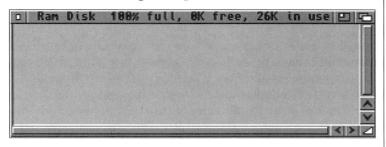

1 Double-click on the Ram Disk icon to open a window.

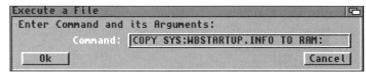

2 Select the "Execute Command..." option from the Workbench menu and type in:

COPY SYS:WBSTARTUP.INFO TO RAM:

then click on "OK".

3 The Ram Disk shows no change from the previous display so now select "Update All" from the Workbench menu.

The changes are now Updated and the new file is visible.

option. To be honest I can't see a great deal of use for this option but it's there if you need it.

Copy

If you drag a file or directory from one device to another the original remains intact and a new copy is made wherever it is placed. However, if you drag from one directory to another on the same device then no copy is made. To duplicate a file on the same device then use the "Copy" option. Thus if a directory called "ThisOne" is copied a new directory called "Copy_of_ThisOne" results. Try it again and a second copy is produced, this time called "Copy_2_of_ThisOne". Anything within the directory is also copied.

Rename...

Guess what this one does! It has one neat sophistication in that it doesn't panic if you select several icons at once. Instead it presents their names one-by-one for amendment.

Information...

This is one of the more powerful options. The information it displays relates to a file's size, its type, the status of its file protection flags, when it was last updated and keeps a record of any associated Tool Types and Filenotes. Not only this, it allows most of these details to be altered and resaved.

Snapshot

Just like the Windows "Snapshot" option this makes a record of where an icon is displayed. So, if you want the Workbench disk to be displayed in the bottom righthand corner of the screen on Startup simply move it there and Snapshot it.

Unsnapshot

When you've realised that you didn't want to Snapshot an icon this reverses the damage.

Leave Out

This is quite a handy option particularly for hard drive owners. Let's say that you are a heavy user of the Shell then it is useful to have the icon near to hand for those many occasions when you need to use it. Click on its icon and then on "Leave Out" and it is automatically dragged from its directory and placed on the desktop. It is no longer necessary to keep the System directory on the Workbench disk open.

The program is still being stored in the same place but its icon has moved to where you can get to it more easily.

Put Away

This puts away any icon that has previously been Left Out.

Delete...

This deletes any selected icon or icons. Thankfully it offers a failsafe device in the form of a pop-up window asking you to confirm your decision. Most of the time this is a nuisance – "Yes, of course, I want to delete those files that's why I selected the Delete option!" – but it's the one time in a hundred that it saves the day.

Format Disk...

This works in the same way as the Format utility in the System directory mainly because it is just another way of using it. It not only formats disks but also presents a variety of ways in which this can be done. The format options are Trashcan, Fast File System, International Mode and Directory Cache. Each of these options has a "toggle" switch next to it which can either be switched on (as signified by a tick or check) or off (blank).

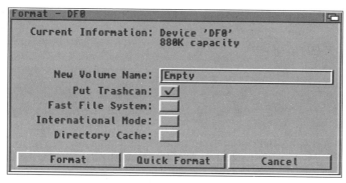

Figure 1.1. The Format disk window.

The Trashcan option determines whether or not you want to use the Trashcan as a means of deleting files. It's there by default but many users will find it superfluous.

The next three options – Fast File System, International Mode and Directory Cache – are all desirable albeit with one proviso. Fast File System lets the Amiga fit more information onto a floppy disk and makes that disk quicker to use than before. International Mode "corrects a case-sensitivity problem associated with international characters" according to Commodore so look into this only if you are using foreign characters in your filenames etc. Directory Caching improves the speed of opening directories and so on. In normal use then, all three options should be "on". The drawback is that disks so formatted won't work with Amigas or Amiga Workbench software before Release 2 and, in the case of Directory Caching before Release 3.

Once the options are set, formatting is a question of choosing "Format" or "Quick Format". Choose the latter if the disk has previously been formatted as an Amiga disk because it is much more rapid.

Empty Trash

The Trashcan is the other way of deleting files. When formatting disks you can decide whether or not you want to keep this icon on. The Trashcan acts just like any other directory except that it cannot itself be deleted from the Workbench. To delete a file just drag it over the Trashcan directory and let go. The analogy with a trash can is very apt because if you change your mind about throwing something away you can rescue it from the Trashcan. Double-click on its icon and all the trash is there ready to be rescued. And, unlike a real life trashcan any rescued files do not come out smelling of last night's dinner. The analogy can be stretched one stage further – once the trash has been emptied it is gone for good. On the A1200 that is done by selecting the "Empty Trash" option.

Tool Menu

The Tools menu is used primarily to host functions associated with software written to use it. This is normally software that doesn't require an on-screen icon. In its raw format the Workbench Tools menu contains just the ResetWB option.

Short-cuts

Most of the options on the menus above have a hot-key shortcut associated with them. It's just another way of selecting an option so for example the "Execute Command..." option can be invoked by holding down the righthand <Amiga> key and then pressing the letter <E>. With frequently used options this is faster than the mouse and pointer method. Potentially "dangerous"

Insider Guide #2: Tidying up with Hot Keys.

Drag a few items from the Workbench disk onto the Ram Disk. They tend to end up scattered any which way.

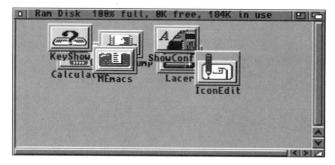

To tidy up the display simply hold down the righthand <Amiga> key and then press the following three keys in sequence:

<.>

<A>

<S>

The <Amiga><.> hot-key combination tidies up the contents of a window.

<Amiga><A> selects the contents of the window and <Amiga><S> saves the positions of the items within the window. To verify this close the Ram Disk window and re-open it to see the position of the various icons.

options such as Delete don't have a short-cut so there's no fear of accidentally hitting the wrong combination.

Hot-key	Function
<Amiga>A	Select contents of window
<Amiga>B	Toggle Workbench window On/Off
<Amiga>C	Make copy of selected icon
<Amiga>E	Opens the "Execute Command…" window
<Amiga>I	Display information about selected icon
<Amiga>K	Close current window
<Amiga>L	Leave out icon on the Workbench
<Amiga>N	Create New drawer in selected window
<Amiga>O	Open selected icon ie open drawer or launch program
<Amiga>P	Put away item previously left out – undoes <Amiga>L
<Amiga>Q	Quit Workbench
<Amiga>R	Rename selected icon: disk, directory, program etc
<Amiga>S	Snapshot position of selected icon
<Amiga>U	Unsnapshot - undo effect of <Amiga>S
<Amiga>?	Provide information About versions
<Amiga>.	Tidy up visible contents of selected window

Table 1.1. Amiga menu hot-key shortcuts.

2

Control the way in which your Workbench operates by using all the goodies which you can find on the Extras disk.

Extras! Extras! Read all about it...

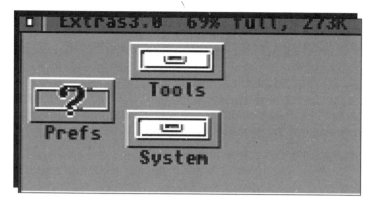

*T*he Extras disk is well worth a little exploration. It contains many items that are useful in setting-up Workbench but which aren't used in the day to day process.

For example, you may well wish to alter the physical appearance (or sound!) of your standard Workbench or you may want to tweak the way in which it behaves. One of the benefits of the Workbench system is that it has been designed to let you do just that. Most of the equipment you will need to do that job can be found on the Extras disk in the Preferences directory. By that I mean that if, for example, you want to alter the colour or change the sound that the A1200 makes when it beeps at you, then you will need to use the Preferences program on the Extras disk. But once you have made those choices they are then stored on your Workbench disk and there is no need to use Extras again. Or at least not until you want to change something else.

The Tools directory contains a variety of programs of varying usefulness. If any one of them is one you cannot live without then it is as well to copy it across onto your Workbench disk. If there's no room for it there then now is the time to consider what you have on your Workbench disk that you can cheerfuly live without – the Clock, perhaps – and swap the two around.

Also on the Extras disk is a System directory which contains the "Intellifont" utility. Another invaluable beasty, this is covered in more depth in Chapter Six which is all about fonts.

Preferences

There is many a fine hour that can be spent toying with the design of the A1200's Graphical User Interface (or GUI for short) all of which is a grand way of saying *the bit you see*. To enable you to do just this the Amiga contains a wide variety of simple, but highly useful windows called Preference Editors. These are located in the Prefs drawer on the Extras disk and each can be opened simply by double-clicking on the icon you require.

The Preference editors allow you to alter virtually all of the standard functions of the Amiga – or more correctly the way the Amiga relates to you the user.

For instance try this: select the Ram Disk by clicking once on its icon and then select "Leave Out" from the Workbench "Icons" menu. The screen flashes, the machine beeps and a frosty little message saying:

Cannot 'Leave Out' this icon

appears acros the top of the screen. Well you knew that, the Ram Disk is already *out*, it can't be left any more out than that and nor, for that matter, can it be Put Away. This sort of beeping and flashing is a standard on the A1200 when you make a mistake but like everything else it can be tailored to your needs. The *Insider Guide* opposite shows you how to go about this.

If you work through the example, with the A1200 beeping away to its heart's content you can start playing around with the beep's volume, pitch or length. Find a combination that you like and you can save the settings to your Workbench disk by selecting "Save" and then following the disk swapping instructions. Alternatively you can choose "Use" which will use that sound for the rest of this computing session but as soon as you switch off or soft-reboot, it will revert to its default settings.

Insider Guide #3: Sound Preferences.

Find the "Sound" tool which is in the Prefs directory of the Extras disk.

Double-clicking on its icon brings up a window headed "Sound Preferences".

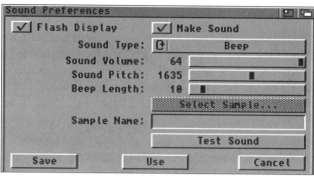

This presents the controls for adjusting the noise the machine makes to report an error. To produce that sound just click on the "Test Sound" button. If at this point you have no sound then one of two things is wrong:

a) the "Make Sound" option is switched off. Click on its button to alter its state. Or:

b) you aren't wired up for sound. The A1200 itself doesn't have a speaker but relies on being connected to an appropriate sound generator. In most cases this will be the TV screen or monitor you are connected to and it's all a question of turning the volume control up.

The final and most interesting option is to employ a sound file from elsewhere. You can alter its tone, volume and duration but when all's said and done a beep is still a beep. Luckily the beep can be replaced by pretty well any sound you care to mention as long as it is available as an IFF file. It just so happens that such a sound file is available on the companion disk to this book but they are also available by the bucket load from PD libraries, friends, magazine disks etc. For this example I have dragged my chosen sound file across onto the Ram Disk.

To play this sound click on the Beep button. This will now read "Sampled Sound". The next step is to click on "Select Sample..." Doing so brings up another window requesting you to select an IFF Sampled Sound. Mine is on the Ram Disk so I click on the "Volumes" button and then on "Ram Disk" from the list which has presented itself. The sound file I want is at the top of the list so click on that and then click "OK". The request window now disappears and the Sound Preferences window is now showing the file we want. Click on "Test Sound" and play around with the settings as you please. If you don't like this sample then find one that suits.

At this point we need to consider what happens when the Workbench starts up. It goes through all that whirring and then discovers that it has to load a sound file that it doesn't know about and so it complains about it: "Error: can't load sound: Ram Disk:soundfile". So any defaults that are to be incorporated into the Startup procedure must be included on the Workbench disk itself. The simplest procedure then is to create a new directory on the Workbench disk called "Bits" and to put any such files into it.

The final option in this Preference is that of "Flash Display". I recommend you leave this toggled "on". This makes the screen flicker once when an error is reported and is a useful backup when the sound is switched off for example.

All the other Preference editors work in very much the same way and you can have a great deal of fun playing around and experimenting with them. The more popular ones are described below – if you want a fully worked example of each then I would recommend you get hold of a copy of *Mastering Amiga Workbench* 3 by Bruce Smith.

Font

Lets you choose the fonts that form all or part of the Workbench display. Separate options can be made for the Workbench Icon Text, the System Default Text and the text within screens. You can also choose which colours you want all the Workbench Icon Text to appear in. The default setting is for black text on a grey background but you may, for example, find dark blue on pale yellow more restful on the eye. The number of colours you get to choose from is dictated by the screen mode you are in and the number of colours you have chosen.

Note: you will get unusual and unsatisfactory results if you save the settings for a screen mode with more colours than that which you use by default. Try it and see what I mean.

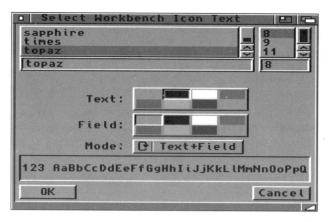

Figure 2.1. The Workbench Icon Text screen showing colour possibilities.

Input

This option controls how you put your input into the machine and offers several hepful options. Mouse Speed predictably refers to the speed at which the mouse propels the pointer. Set it to three and it fair whizzes around, set it to one and you need a desk the size of Kent. The best compromise is to select two and have the "Acceleration" option switched on. This rather elegant feature makes the pointer movement respond to the speed with which you move the mouse. Move it quickly and the pointer leaps around but move it slowly and you have quite delicate control. That's my choice but of course you may prefer something else.

The Double-click delay option controls the time in which you are allowed to make the second click before the machine decides that it wasn't a double-click after all but two separate single clicks. It isn't a good idea to set this too fast otherwise you'll never get anything done. The Keyboard settings control how the keys respond when you are typing. If you are using a wordprocessor, holding down a letter makes it repeat until released. This option sets the defaults for that and is very much a matter of playing round with it until it suits your needs.

The righthand window shows the keyboard options. This lists all the keyboard maps that are to be found in the SYS:Devs/Keymaps directory *plus* the default setting "American". Click on the one you want to use and then on "Save". If the one you want isn't there then it needs to be loaded into the SYS:Devs/Keymaps directory from the Keymaps directory on the Storage disk.

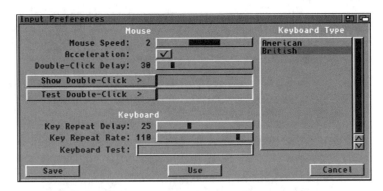

Figure 2.2. The Input Preferences editor.

Locale

Si, par example, tu parle Francais...

If you don't understand English you can change the language the A1200 uses in its display with the Locale option which collects the text from the "Locale" disk. But then, if you don't understand English, how did you read this to find that out?

Locale also supplies a very pretty scrolling map of the world with all the time zones marked on. If you find a practical use for this, you will let me know, won't you?

Overscan

Controls the physical area of the screen that Workbench occupies. Two modes are offered: Graphics and Text. You may wish to set different limits dependent on the application you are using. Most monitors have a discernible curvature to them which is strongest nearest the edges of the screen. Reducing the Overscan area reduces the effect on the screen image of this distortion. Conversely, when you want the display to be as large as you can get it, Overscan can be used to overlap with the edges of the monitor. Adjustments are made by dragging one of the black boxes. The central box can be used to set the position on-screen of the complete image.

Palette

You could play all day with this and still fail to come up with the perfect colours for the appearance of your Workbench screen. My tip would be to be sparing in your use of dayglo colours unless you actually enjoy having to wear a pair of shades while using your computer.

Like most of these Preference tools "Palette" has a "Restore to Defaults" option amongst its menu choices and this can be a godsend.

Pointer

Another customising tool, this one lets you design your own pointer icon. Should you wish, you can even load an icon you have created elsewhere by using the "Load Image" option from the Edit menu. I expect that, as with many of these Workbench options, you will probably end up using the original default options.

Printer, PrinterGfx and PrinterPS

These three options govern the appearance of the printed output. They are discussed in more detail in Chapter 12 – Print Out.

ScreenMode

This comprehensive option controls how many colours are used on a particular screen, the dimensions of the Workbench window and the relative size of all the icons and windows that appear on a screen. It deserves a chapter of its own, and gets one – Put It On Display.

Serial

Connecting two computers, often via a telephone line, is not as difficult as it might seem. As long as they present each other with data in an agreed format and don't try to speak when the other one's talking then there should be no problems. In practice, if you are using a modem then the software that comes with it or that you have bought for it should be able to control these settings more satisfactorily.

Time

Not surprisingly this is used to set the date and time. However, unless you have a battery-backed clock fitted to your A1200 – something that doesn't come with the standard machine – this is going to be of limited use. On a brighter note it did let me find out that Christmas is on a Monday in the year 2000.

WBPattern

Another means of prettying up the appearance of the A1200 GUI. You can for example have a picture to form the background to the Workbench or any window if you so wish. In much the same way that a sampled sound was chosen in the "Sound" Preference so it can with a Picture. Again, to be of practical use this picture needs to be stored on the Workbench disk to be available at startup.

All

All the Preference options offer the chance to save a particular group of settings. This is stored in the Workbench:Prefs/Presets file. Several different settings can be saved here allowing you to choose which one you want to use on any one occasion. For example you might want to use an interlaced mode with only a few screen colours when using a DTP program, a low-res screen mode with lots of colours when working with a paint package and a high-res screen with eight colours for wordprocessing. Storing Preference settings from one of these Prefs programs lets you do exactly that.

IControl

See Chapter 14 "Put It On Display".

Tools Drawer

The Tools drawer holds a useful – if not oddball – variety of programs that provide you with a degree of productivity when it comes to using your Amiga. Here's a round-up of what they are.

Calculator

It's nothing more than the simplest sort of calculator but it can come in handy. The Public Domain is stuffed with similar programs that are vastly superior.

CMD, Graphic Dump, InitPrinter and PrintFiles

CMD allows you to print to a file, GraphicDump prints out a copy of whatever is on screen, InitPrinter tells the printer about the preferences you have set and PrintFiles is a rough and ready way of printing out plain text files. These programs are covered in more depth in the Print Out chapter.

IconEdit

Chapter 10 "MORE AmigaDOS" shows how to create your own application. Doing this produces an application which has an icon associated with it identical to the Shell utility. Using IconEdit you can change this to any appearance you care to draw.

Keyshow

Shows how different ASCII symbols can be obtained by the combination of a key press and the <Amiga>, <Ctrl> and <Shift> keys. Keys

Insider Guide #4: Background pictures.

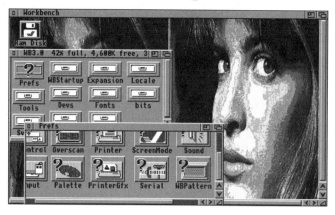

Select the picture that you want to use as a background display. Place it on your Workbench disk so that it is available on startup.

Open WBPattern from the prefs directory on the Extras disk. Click on the Type gadget until it displays Picture and then click on the Select Picture gadget which was previously not made available.

This pops up a file requester. Work through the options until you find the picture file that you wish to use. Click on "OK" which returns you to the original window. Click on "Test" to see whether it creates the desired effect. If it does, "Use" will retain it for the current session whilst "Save" makes it a permanent feature of the Workbench display.

displayed with a tilde symbol (~) have no effect, whilst those with a caret symbol (^) describe an action such as "Delete" or "Return". Not immediately useful you may think but invaluable within an ASCII document for describing layouts etc.

Lacer

When working on video editing with a genlock attached to the back of the A1200 it can be useful to be able to switch between screen modes. "Lacer" is designed to permit toggling (swapping) between one mode and its interlaced version. It only works when a genlock is attached.

MEMACS

This is a text editor along the same lines as ED but it is much more sophisticated. It offers many features and it's a matter of debate whether or not you can call this kind of text editor a wordprocessor. Its facilities are discussed further in the *MORE AmigaDOS* chapter.

PrepCard

This controls the use of RAM cards in the PCMCIA slot which can be found on the lefthand side of the A1200. It is described in detail in the "Improve Your Memory" chapter.

ShowConfig

ShowConfig is of technical interest only. It provides information on the processor being used, the custom chips, the VERSION numbers of Workbench and Kickstart being used and detects the presence of any RAM upgrade or hardware boards. You are unlikely to need it except when purchasing hardware add-ons when the existing configuration of your machine may be important in choosing the right version of the add-on. Be ready to quote these details when shopping.

Commodities

There are eight of these handy little tools in all. They work in the background and can make the routine use of the Workbench that much easier. To see what each does launch the Commodities Exchange program.

Exchange

This is the Big Daddy of these utilities. It shows any currently selected Commodities and also any other programs that have been launched from the WBStartup directory. Clicking on the name of a Commodity in the Available Commodities list gives a brief description of each one. They can also be rendered active or inactive via the Commodities Exchange window which is an effective way of controlling your choices.

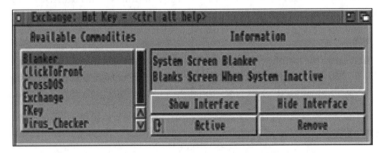

Figure 2.3. The Exchange window.

The Commodities take up very little room on the Workbench disk. It's a matter of taste which, if any, you use but Blanker should not be overlooked.

AutoPoint

Click in a window and it becomes active as signified by the blue border around that window. AutoPoint cuts out this stage and automatically highlights the window beneath the mouse pointer.

Blanker

Protects the monitor from the damage of burn-in. A static screen display will eventually carve its way onto the screen leaving its ghostly presence behind as a permanent reminder. Blanker helps reduce the damage by switching off the normal display when there has been no keyboard or mouse input for a specified length of time.

ClickToFront

With several windows open at once it is often difficult to bring the one you want to the front of the stack. With ClickToFront active you just need to double-click in the desired window whilst holding down the <Alt> key and it comes to the top of the heap.

CrossDOS

The CrossDOS utility helps pass information between the Amiga and MS-DOS machines (IBM-compatible PCs). Although all computers accept certain file types as standard – ASCII, for example – there remain subtle differences between them. CrossDOS helps smooth over these differences.

FKey

This is a real *love it or hate it* utility. It lets you manipulate the size of windows, their relative positions, the relative positions of screens, run programs or ARexx scripts and use shortcuts in typing all by using just a few keys on the keyboard. The only difficulty is remembering which key does what. Get it wrong and you'll have programs launching themselves left, right and centre and then disappearing somewhere behind a mess of rapidly shrinking and expanding windows!

MouseBlanker

A very subtle one this one, so subtle you might almost call it useless. It makes the pointer disappear whenever you are entering text, only to reappear when the mouse is moved.

NoCapsLock

Also of limited use, this disables the <Caps Lock> key. If you're a particularly clumsy typist you might find A USE FOR IT.

No Popup

By default the AutoPoint, ClickToFront, MouseBlanker and NoCapsLock commodities launch themselves as background tasks. Which means that when you boot up you never get to see them, they just load somewhere in the background and get on with it; which is what you want. By contrast the Blanker, CrossDOS, FKey and Exchange programs all open windows on the Workbench where you can set the parameters by which they work. As you won't want to do this every time you boot up it is better to alter their default settings to prevent them from opening a window.

Click on the relevant icon to highlight the commodity, then select Information from the Workbench Icons menu.

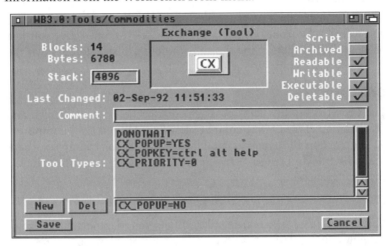

In the "Tool Types" window highlight the CX_POPUP=YES line and this will then be displayed in the little window beneath. Adjust it so that it reads CX_POPUP=NO and then click on "Save".

Insider Guide #5: Function key shortcuts.

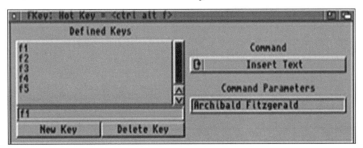

Open the FKey utiltity which is found in the Commodities>>Tools directory on the Extras disk. Click on "New Key"and type in the characters: "F" and "1".

Click on theCommand gadget until "Toggle Window Size" is displayed. Click on New Key and this time enter <F><2>. Now select "Insert Text" and enter your name in the "Command parameters". box.

Select "Save..." from the menu options. Now open a Shell window and press the function keys F1 and F2. You should see the window enlarge and then display your name.

FKey can also be used to launch programs and scripts, to cycle through windows and to alter their size.

**AmigaDOS is at the very heart of the A1200.
Find out how it beats...**

```
┌─┐ AmigaShell
New Shell process 4
4.Workbench3.0:> LIST #?.INFO TO RAM:LISTFILE
4.Workbench3.0:> TYPE RAM:LISTFILE
Devs.info                        632 ----rw-d Today
Expansion.info                   632 ----rw-d Today
Prefs.info                       724 ----rw-d Today
System.info                      632 ----rw-d Today
Utilities.info                   632 ----rw-d Today
WBStartup.info                   632 ----rw-d Today
Disk.info                        388 ----rw-d Today
7 files - 20 blocks used
4.Workbench3.0:> █
```

*I*f you haven't come to terms with AmigaDOS yet, then now is the time for a little exploration. Set aside a few hours for practice and you will surprise yourself with how easy it can be to produce simple utilities on the A1200. The first book in this series introduced several AmigaDOS commands and showed how they could be used to speed up your computing. These are explained below with some examples that may be useful.

Getting Going

To start using AmigaDOS, double-click on the Shell icon that is found in the System directory of the Workbench disk. This opens the window where you can enter your commands.

AmigaDOS can be used as an alternative to the Workbench screen. All the facilities that Workbench lets you do: moving files around, copying them, deleting them, creating new directories, running programs and so on can also be done using AmigaDOS commands. The reason for the duplication is that the Workbench *front end*, as it's called, is very quick and easy to use. You can see at a glance where everything is and for most purposes it is quicker. To launch a program from the Workbench means a double-click of the mouse button. To do the same in AmigaDOS requires typing in the program's name along with the directories it is in and a command to RUN.

The advantage that AmigaDOS offers is that it can provide quick access to more information and it can be used to write script files. These are several AmigaDOS commands put together in one file. Once the file has been written there is no need to repeat typing the commands over and over again. Instead the file can be run and all the work will be done for you.

At Your Command...

AmigaDOS commands have been designed so that their use and meaning is as obvious as possible. If you want to run a program the command is RUN, to delete a file, type DELETE and so on.

Filing Cabinets

The first group of commands are mainly concerned with file manipulation. There is little here that cannot be performed with greater ease from the Workbench. However, they do form the basis for future AmigaDOS programming. Open the Shell and type in the examples below.

DIR

On its own DIR provides a list of the entire contents of the current directory. Used with a directory name after it shows the contents of that directory. It isn't limited to cataloguing the entire contents of a directory either. Writing a *modifier* after it enables only specified file types to be displayed.

Try the following commands to see how it works:

```
DIR

DIR S

DIR DIRS

DIR RAM: FILES

DIR #?.INFO
```

DIR S#?

If the output from this command is too prodigious and flashes past too quickly then the process can be halted by pressing the space bar. Hitting return gets it going again. The #?.INFO option used above lists all the files that end with those five characters. Similarly DIR S#? lists all the files beginning with the letter S. The #? characters are referred to as wildcards and this process is called pattern matching.

LIST

It's amazing that such a seemingly simple command can be so complex. LIST behaves in much the same way as DIR except that it is more powerful. On its own LIST provides a similar breakdown of information but also supplies data about the physical size of files, information about file flags (See Chapter Seven, *The Protection Racket*) and the date the file was last updated (if you are lucky enough to have an internal clock on your A1200). You can limit yourself to just directories or files in the same way:

LIST S

LIST DIRS

LIST FILES

LIST #?.INFO

To reveal the contents of each and every directory try

LIST ALL

However, as this can take forever with the Workbench disk the best thing to do is to hit <Ctrl><C> and the process is stopped. LIST can also produce an output:

LIST TO RAM:FILELIST

produces a file on the Ram Disk called 'FILELIST' which holds all the details that would normaly be sent to the Shell window.

MAKEDIR

MAKEDIR is used to create a new directory. It differs from the New Drawer command on the Workbench in that no .info file associated with the directory is made. This is perhaps the simplest way of differentiating between directories and drawers – the absence or presence of .info files. MAKEDIR can be used to make a new directory wherever specified. You can only make directories one at a time. If you want a sequence of directories/subdirectories like the following:

RAM:PLANTS/TREES/DECIDUOUS

then it has to be created a directory at a time. But, if you use the arrow up key on the keyboard after each command then the following sequence will be almost as quick:

MAKEDIR RAM:PLANTS

MAKEDIR RAM:PLANTS/TREES

MAKEDIR RAM:PLANTS/TREES/DECIDUOUS

DELETE

A certain amount of caution is advisable when using this command for the obvious reason. Delete the wrong file and you're going to feel pretty stupid. Pattern matching can be used but this only increases the potential for disaster – it's all too easy to erase a few extra files that you had forgotten about or didn't even know existed:

DELETE RAM:PLANTS/TREES

doesn't work because the directory "TREES" isn't empty. AmigaDOS takes the cautious approach and prevents you from accidentally erasing large volumes of data. Using the "ALL" suffix acknowledges that there is data in the directory and everything will be deleted. ALL can, therefore, be very useful and, by the same token, very disruptive:

DELETE RAM:PLANTS/TREES ALL

COPY

COPY copies a file or files. It can be used to copy several files at once:

1> COPY A|B|C RAM:

Will copy files A, B and C from the current directory onto the Ram Disk. Directories can also be copied like so:

1> COPY FROM A: TO RAM:B

This copies the directory A and its contents across to the Ram Disk renaming it as it does so. Try it and see; the Ram Disk should contain a new directory "B" which is otherwise a direct copy of the previous "A" directory.

DISKCOPY

DISKCOPY is the fastest way to duplicate disks and is invaluable for making back-up copies of your Workbench disks! It can be a slow process with just the one floppy disk drive but, as we shall find out later, there are ways around that. Until then the command:

```
1> DISKCOPY DF0: DF0:
```

should be sufficient. What this command is saying is copy the disk in drive DF0: onto the other disk in drive DF0:. "How do I get two disks in one disk drive ?" I hear you ask. The answer is you don't. The A1200 will instruct you when you are to insert the SOURCE disk (the one you are copying FROM) and when to insert the DESTINATION disk (the one you are copying TO).

Owners of two floppy drives have life easy:

```
1> DISKCOPY DF0: DF1:
```

copies from DF0: to DF1: – just make sure you put the right disk in the right drive! Write-protecting your SOURCE disk is also a wise idea.

CD

CD means "Change Directory" and it does just that. A command like:

```
CD SYS:Tools
```

changes the current directory to the Tools directory on the System disk. Using the:

```
CD /
```

command moves up the directory tree to the directory one above it. In this case the SYS: disk main directory. The current directory is the one whose name appears before the cursor prompt eg:

```
1.Workbench3.0:>
```

or

```
Ram Disk:>
```

RELABEL

RELABEL is one of AmigaDOS's renaming commands and is used to rename devices. These include floppy disks, the Ram Disk, the RAD disk, hard drive partitions etc. The syntax of this command is along the lines of:

```
1> RELABEL DRIVE DF0: NAME "New Name"
```

or

```
1> RELABEL "Old Name": "New Name"
```

RENAME

Like RELABEL but this command applies to files and directories. So, for example, you might say:

```
1> RENAME RAM:DIR/FILE "RAM:DIR/NEW NAME"
```

which finds FILE in the DIR directory on the Ram Disk and calls it NEW NAME. The only real complication with this command is in the use of quoatation marks. Notice how they go round the complete name of the file in question if it is to include spaces – this applies whether it is the old file name, the new name or both.

FORMAT

FORMAT initialises a new disk in the relevant format. Typically it will be used in the:

```
1> FORMAT DRIVE DF0: NAME "MyDisk"
```

style. There are various options to go with the format command: such as FFS, NOICONS and QUICK. FFS uses the Fast Filing System option and NOICONS prevents the appearance of the Trashcan directory. QUICK can be used to reformat a disk that has already been formatted. It's a quick way of wiping unwanted data but should only be used with disks that are known to be "healthy".

Writing Scripts

A script is just another word for *program*. Computer programming always has an aura of mystique to it but, when using AmigaDOS, this is unfounded. It really couldn't be easier. The A1200 comes supplied with a text editor appropriately enough called ED. ED can be used to write a list of AmigaDOS commands in a file. This file can be saved and used at a later date when its commands are carried out in sequence.

ED

To create a new script, called "Test" in ED just type in:

```
ED TEST
```

This pops up a new window where the script can be written and saved. Saving is done by pressing the Esc key followed by X. The file "Test" will be saved to the current directory which, at this stage, will probably be the root directory of the Workbench disk. A more suitable place would be on the Ram Disk so the first command could be rewritten as:

Insider Guide #6: Writing a script in ED.

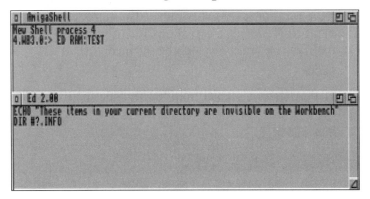

Create a new script file from the Shell by typing in

ED RAM:TEST

This opens a second window in ED, the A1200's text processor. Script writing is now just a question of typing in the commands and saving. For the sake of this simple example type in:

ECHO "These are the items visible on the Workbench in your current directory:"

DIR #?.INFO

To save the program press the <Esc> key followed by <X>. This returns you to the Shell. Now type in:

EXECUTE RAM:TEST

to reveal a listing of the visible items within your current directory.

ED RAM:TEST

There are several commands for manipulating text within ED all of which are preceded by the Esc button. A complete list of these ED commands can be found in Figure 3.1. ED can also be used to examine and update a file that already exists, eg:

ED S:STARTUP-SEQUENCE

EXECUTE

Nothing to do with assassination, EXECUTE is used to run script files. For example, the "TEST" file used in the previous paragraph could be run by typing in:

EXECUTE TEST

RUN

RUN is similar to EXECUTE except that it is used to launch programs
rather than AmigaDOS script files. When launching a program from
the Shell the RUN command isn't always strictly necessary. The Clock,
for example, can be launched simply by entering:

```
CLOCK
```

However this *freezes* the Shell from further input until the Clock is
closed. Use:

```
RUN CLOCK
```

and both processes can run alongside each other.

ECHO

Is a simple way of passing comment. Included in an AmigaDOS script
it can be used to prompt action from the user eg:

```
ECHO "Put the SOURCE disk in drive DF0:"
```

asks the user to do just that. Insider Guide #6 uses ECHO to explain to
the user the meaning of the data being displayed.

Miscellany

There are well over 100 AmigaDOS
commands, so it is nigh on impossible to cover them all here.
Therefore, I have included brief descriptions of the more interesting
ones that you might like to experiment with. If you want a real inside
guide to AmigaDOS then check out *Mastering AmigaDOS 3 Tutorial*
and *A to Z Reference* by Mark Smiddy.

ALIAS

As its name suggests, ALIAS provides another renaming service. Not
for file names or device names this time but as a shortcut to save having to type in lengthy commands that you use frequently:

```
ALIAS FORMO FORMAT DRIVE DF0: NAME "[]"
FORMO BLANK DISK
```

In this example the FORMAT command has been shortened. The
square brackets [] indicate that a variable is to be inserted when the
ALIASed command is used. With this in place there is no need for the
use of inverted commas for the NAME given to the formatted disk.

Use of the ALIAS command on its own shows all the currently used ALIASes. These include CLEAR which is just an ECHO command.

ASSIGN

ASSIGN is remarkably similar to the ALIAS command except that it is used to provide abbreviations for PATH names.

For example, if you commonly use:

```
TOOLS/UTILITIES
```

this can be abbreviated to, say:

```
UTIL
```

if the A1200 has been informed that UTIL is the assignation for that particular directory. The way in which this notification is made is by:

```
ASSIGN UTIL: DF0:TOOLS/UTILITIES
```

There's no end to the number of ways ASSIGN can be used but its usefulness does rely on you remembering what has been ASSIGNed to what. Alternatively you can remind yourself by typing in ASSIGN on its own which brings up the complete list of ASSIGNed commands.

DATE

This allows the date and time to be written or read. Entered on its own it returns the default setting, whatever that is, or it can be used to reset that information in the:

```
DATE DD-MMM-YY HH:MM:SS
```

format. Thus, to change the date and time to half past ten in the evening on the 26th of July, 1994 use this style:

```
DATE 26-JUL-94 22:30:00
```

ENDSHELL (ENDCLI)

The two commands do the same thing which is to close the Shell window currently being used. It's not much use on its own – a click on the close gadget is just as effective – but can be invaluably incorporated in scripts which produce output windows.

NEWSHELL (NEWCLI)

This starts a separate Shell process which runs independently from the old one. As the A1200 is a multi-tasking machine several Shells can be up and running at the same time. The command can be used on its own or with a list of numbers which determine where the window is to be positioned on the screen and how large it will be:

NEWSHELL CON:0/100/600/200/SECOND-SHELL/CLOSE

The first two numbers are the x and y cordinates of the top lefthand corner of the new window, the next number is the window's width and then its height. "SECOND-SHELL" is the window's name and the optional CLOSE suffix ensures that the new window has a close gadget

PROMPT

PROMPT customises the Shell PROMPT. In practice you may have little call for this. The default setting is:

PROMPT "%N.%S:> "

where %N gives the Shell process number and %S tells the current directory. The quote marks are used as there is a blank space after the ">" symbol to make things appear tidier.

RESIDENT

RESIDENT is a command which makes no difference to whether a script works or not. If all the RESIDENT commands were stripped from an AmigaDOS script it would still work – so why use it? In a word – speed. RESIDENT places a command in the machine RAM which means that it can be accessed almost instantaneously. In the example

RESIDENT C:ASSIGN

the ASSIGN command is copied from the C: directory on the Workbench disk and stored in machine memory. Every time it is used from now on it is the copy in RAM which is used rather than the one on disk. Typing in RESIDENT on its own lists all those commands that are currently RESIDENT. If a non-resident command is to be used several times within a script then make it resident first to speed things up. The reverse of a RESIDENT command is to use REMOVE. Thus, in the above example, we could use:

RESIDENT ASSIGN REMOVE

which frees up a bit more RAM for other uses.

TYPE

One way of viewing a file is to use the TYPE utility. It is limited in its use in that it spools the contents of that file into the current console window.

TYPE S:STARTUP-SEQUENCE

That's fine if it's a short file but if it's longer than the window then it will scroll past before you've had a chance to look at it properly. The Spacebar stops that scrolling and Return gets it going again.

VERSION

There are only limited uses for VERSION which reads and then displays the Version numbers of the Workbench and Kickstart currently in use. Where it can come in handy is when software requires a certain minimum version number of, say, Workbench to be present before it will operate. As the A1200 is a new machine with a new Workbench, this is not the sort of problem we are likely to encounter for a while.

Wildcards etc

Imagine having a dozen picture files which you want to copy from your *Picture* disk into the Ram Disk. They are called Picture01, Picture02, Picture03 and so on up to Picture12. To copy them across one at a time would be laborious in the extreme but the whole lot can be done with one simple command:

COPY PICTURE#? TO RAM: ALL ;Copies all pictures to RAM

The #? simply denotes that any combination of letters or numbers are acceptable to fill this gap. Thus, any file which has P-I-C-T-U-R-E as its first seven letters will be copied. Too bad if there are extra files copied that you hadn't anticipated. Incidentally the ";Copies all pictures to RAM" part of this command line does absolutely nothing. The semi-colon is used to inform AmigaDOS to ignore anything after that position on the line. When writing scripts of more than just a few lines in length it is a good to get into the habit of writing comments with each important line explaining what each one does so that when you study the program some weeks later trying to adapt it for some other use, you know exactly what does what.

4

Want to see the contents of a file? MultiView lets you display graphics, sound and, of course, text. Look at it this way...

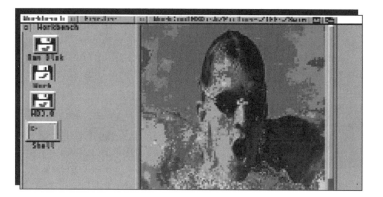

*M*ultiView is a rather aptly named program that comes free with your A1200 – it is to be found in the Utilities directory of the Workbench disk. Its purpose is simply one of letting you view files but its power is quite considerable. Not only can you use it to view text files and pictures but it can also be used to play back sounds and present hypertext documents

To view a text file with MultiView simply double-click on the MultiView icon. A requester headed "Select File to Open" will then come into view asking exactly which file of the dozens available it is that you wish to see. It simultaneously displays the contents of the currently selected directory. Clicking on the "Volumes" button at the bottom of the window allows a choice of disks or, more accurately, devices to be displayed. Click on one of these and the window displays the root directory of that device.

You can now work your way through the various directories and subdirectories by clicking on their names in turn until you reach the file you want. Should you, at any stage, want to go back up the directory "tree" then click on the Parent button.

Eventually you will find the file you want to view. Click on its name and then on the "Open" button. This should open a second window displaying the file you wanted to see. If the file is a text file, a picture file or a hypertext file then the file will be either in text or picture form. If you loaded a sound file then a loudspeaker icon will appear in a window. To have this played just click on the icon.

If you can't hear anything then now is the time to check that your A1200 is correctly wired up. The A1200 doesn't have any internal speakers and relies instead on being attached to a monitor or TV or hi-fi. If it's not linked up it won't play. And if it is linked up but the volume is turned down it still won't play. Yes, I know this all seems painfully obvious now...

It Doesn't Work

MultiView can only display files of a certain type. To find out what types of files you can view, open the Devices directory on your Workbench disk. There are further directories within this one – the one we want is the "DataTypes" directory. Double-clicking on this displays four *file type translations*: 8SVX, AmigaGuide, ILBM and FTXT. What this all means is that MultiView is capable of displaying files which conform to one of these four descriptions. The files within the DataTypes directory are "translations". What they do is supply information about files of those types so that MultiView can display them. It follows that any sort of files can be displayed as long as the appropriate translations is available in "DataTypes". Incidentally the translations themselves are not of a data type that can be read by MultiView. Try and load a file into MultiView that is not of an appropriate type and the program will fail to do so informing you with the message "Unknown date type for..."

However, if your file is of one of the legitimate file types then MultiView will display it in its glory.

MultiView can only display one file at a time but of course your Amiga is a multitasking machine and you can open several MultiView windows should you wish to display more than one.

On the Menu

With MultiView loaded the Menu options available come under four headings: Project, Edit, Window and Settings. Project contains settings such as Print, Quit and Open which allows a new file to be loaded and viewed in preference to the one already present. The About option provides information on the file type that has been loaded.

The Edit menu contains those options for manipulating the information within the file. Depending on the file loaded these options may or may not be active... If the file type is a picture then selecting the Mark option changes the cursor into a crosswires marker. Click and drag a box with this crosswires cursor and an area can be highlighted. This is an excellent way of cropping a picture file to whatever size and shape you want. The Windows menu provides options governing window sizes and the final, Settings menu lets you save any changes you have made as the default settings.

Hyperactivity

The A1200 can process 8SVX sound files, IFF pictures and ASCII text. The fourth option is "AmigaGuide" which sounds interesting, but what is it?

AmigaGuide is a rather elegant way of displaying text in a style normally referred to as *hypertext*. When a normal text file is displayed the scroll bars at the side of the display window allow you to find your way down through several pages worth of text. This is all very well for most purposes but imagine if it were a large document. How would you find the piece of information you were hunting? The AmigaGuide file format is one particular solution to that problem.

What it does is split a document up into separate *pages* with each page containing whatever information the author decides upon. Each page can also be linked to several other pages with the reader making appropriate choices about whichever topic is wanted next.

This approach isn't much use for a conventional novel where the reader is expected to progress linearly from the start through to the announcement that it was, after all, the butler who did it. But for text book purposes it's ideal. Instead of constantly referring the reader to different chapters the author can present various options about which subjects to progress to next. And if you end up exploring a side issue so thoroughly that you get completely off the subject a "Retrace" option allows you to do just that. It keeps a record of the route you have taken through the AmigaGuide maze and lets you retrace your route step by step by repeatedly clicking on the Retrace button.

To view an AmigaGuide document open the MultiView file selector and put the Locale disk into the drive. Work your way down through the directories until you reach:

Locale:Help/english/sys/amigaguide.guide

Open this file and a window with buttons on it appears. Try clicking on these buttons and you'll rapidly come to terms with how these guides can be used.

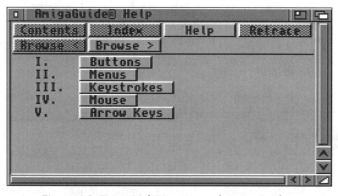

Figure 4.1. Using MultiView to read AmigaGuides.

Dungeon Text

As progress through an AmigaGuide document can be like negotiating a maze I have constructed just such an item. It's called "Dungeon" and is available on the Next Steps Disk. It is also included in full at the end of this chapter for scrutiny and as a means for inspiring you to write your own hypertext documents.

"Welcome to the Dungeon" it says. Yes, welcome indeed, all you need to do is read the text on each page, digest the information supplied and set off in search of gold. Each page presents you with a variety of highlighted options mainly concerning where to go next. Click on one of these options and you turn to a new page. The game consists of a dungeon of twelve rooms all linked to each other by passageways. The object is to negotiate a route through The Dungeon to The Bullion Room without dying. I'll leave you to explore The Dungeon for yourself.

This example was only intended to serve as an example of MultiView's capabilities. As you will quickly realise, it lacks a great deal as a games-playing medium because if you make the wrong move it allows you to retrace your steps – that "Retrace" button once again. Not only that but you can look through each page or Room simply by clicking on one of the browse Buttons at the top of the screen. Furthermore you can return to the starting point at any time by clicking on the "Contents" button.

Getting it together

Writing "Dungeon" was simplicity itself. It was all done in ED and took a good hour at most.

From the Shell create an ED file called "Dungeon":

```
ED DUNGEON
```

Once in ED the first requirement is to write a file header so that when MultiView tries to display it, it knows what sort of document it is faced with. In this case:

```
@database
```

is quite sufficient. Our next requirement is to choose the "wordwrap" display option so that the text does just that:

```
@wordwrap
```

From here it is just a question of creating as many pages as you require. Each page must start with a header identifying it as a new page and with a name by which MultiView can identify it, for instance:

```
@node "Room1"
```

In the Dungeon example each page gives information about a different room in the dungeon. No surprise then that I have named them "Room1", "Room2", "Room3" and so on. The exception to this is the first page to be displayed which must go under the name of "MAIN".

These names are the names by which MultiView recognises them. However, they needn't be the names which the user has to face. If you wish to give the pages a different title then the command:

```
@title "Screen Title"
```

should be used. Whatever is written within the quote marks will be what appears on the top of that page of the MultiView document. The end of each page should similarly be signified with the:

```
@endnode
```

command.

The start of "Dungeon" looks like this:

```
@database
@wordwrap
@node MAIN
@title "The Dungeon"
@ endnode
@node Room1
@title "The Crypt"
@endnode
@node Room2
@title "The Library"
@endnode
@node Room3
@title "The Banqueting Hall"
@endnode
```

etc...

So far so good. This produces a MultiView document with several blank pages but no text. The next task is to type in the storyline to be displayed on each page. For example "This is the Crypt but it's not very cryptic..." and so on. Finally we need a way of linking the pages to each other. The best way of doing this is to have various words on each page highlighted so that the user can click on them and turn to the relevant page.

In the Dungeon example we want to have a statement such as "there is a passageway to the West" with the word "West" highlighted so that clicking on it moves us from the room we are on to whatever is at the end of the route to the west. In MultiView this is simplicity itself. When writing the text for each page any words can be easily highlighted as follows:

```
@{"West" link Room3}
```

this places the word "West" in a little box. When the player clicks in this box he is taken from that room to Room3.

Other Uses

Of course a second-rate adventure game is only one example of how this sort of database might be of use. As an educational document it could be used to store information on, say, trees. Each page could contain information about a particular species with buttons arranged so that additional information on certain aspects can be accessed or so that shared information could be viewed.

AmigaDOS 3

MultiView can also be launched from the Shell or the "Execute Command" option on the Workbench. The syntax for this command is:

MULTIVIEW FILENAME

but in the case of graphics this restrains you to displaying in the current screen mode. If you use the suffix SCREEN as in:

MULTIVIEW FILENAME SCREEN

then a new screen is produced and the picture can be displayed in all its colour without being restricted by the choice of colours available to whatever screen mode has been configured.

Command	Description
@database	Informs MultiView what sort of document is being used.
@wordwrap	Switches on the automatic word wrap facility.
@MAIN	The opening page.
@node ...	The start of any other page.
@title "Name"	Gives a page the title of "Name".
@{"Button" link Elsewhere}	Creates a highlighted button. When this is pressed the linking facility takes the user to the "Elsewhere" page.
@endnode	Defines the end of any individual page.
@{b}	Bold on.
@{ub}	Bold off.
@{i}	Italics on.
@{ui}	Italics off.
@{u}	Underlining on.
@{uu}	Underlining off.

Table 4.1. The MultiView Commands.

The Dungeon

Owners of the accompanying disk to this volume can play around with a rudimentary adventure game I have created using MultiView. A listing of its text is displayed below:

```
@database

@wordwrap

@node MAIN

@title "Dungeon"

Welcome to the Dungeon. It's not very complicated
and even less scary. You are in the main entrance
room, facing north. There is an exit straight
ahead and a rope dangling from the ceiling. Which
way do you want to go?

@{b}Remember:@{ub} Secrets get you nowhere.

@{"North" link Room1}
```

Insider Guide #7: Editing a picture.

With your Workbench disk loaded, double-click with the lefthand mouse button on the MultiView icon from the "Utilities" directory to launch the program.

When the file requester is displayed, work through the appropriate directories to find the IFF picture you want. Click on the "Open" button. The picture will be displayed on screen in its own file viewer.

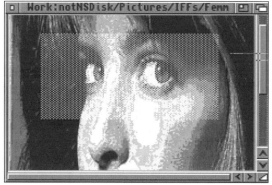

From the menu options select "Mark". Position the cursor to the top left of the area you want to select and, holding the left mouse button down, drag the cursor down and right to highlight that complete area. Now release the mouse button. To Save that part of the image select "Save" from the Project menu and enter the name that you wish the image to be saved as.

```
@{"West" link Room2}
@{"Up" link Room3}
@endnode
@node Room1
@title "The Crypt"
```

You find yourself in a dark and dingy room filled with skeletons. It's not too hygienic and a little damp. There is a staircase leading @{"Up" link Room3}, a passageway leading @{"North" link Room5} and a route @{"East" link MAIN}.

@endnode

@node Room2

@title "The Tower"

@{b}Remember:@{ub} You can't fly

@{"Down" link Room1}, @{"North" link Room6}

@endnode

@node Room3

@title The "Vaults"

@{"Down" link Room1}, @{"North" link Room7}, and a Secret Passageway to the @{"East" link Room2}.

@endnode

@node Room4

@title "The Library"

You can tell it's a library because it's full of books. Every time you make the slightest sound one of those I WILL BE OBEYED sort of voices tells you to shut up. @{"North" link Room8}, @{"South" link MAIN}.

@endnode

@node Room5

@title "The Conservatory"

@{"Up" link Room7}, @{"East" link Room4}, @{"Sudden Death" link Death}

@endnode

@node Room6

@title "The Chapel"

It is a chapel and it's full of rather nice golden items. However, you appear to be on a balcony near the roof. There is an exit to the @{"South" link Room2} or you could @{"Jump Down" link Death}.

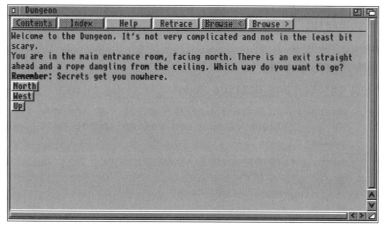

Figure 4.1. The Dungeon screen.

```
@endnode

@node Room7

@title "The Banqueting Hall"

@{"South" link Room3}, @{"Down" link Room5}

@endnode

@node Room8

@title "The Kitchen"

I can't believe they prepare food in here - it's
dirtier than a student house. There is a cake
marked @{"Eat Me" link Death}, a @{"Spiral
Staircase" link Room10} leading upwards, a door
to the @{"West" link Room9} and a passageway to
the @{"South" link Room4}.

@endnode

@node Room9

@title "The Study"

@{"Secret Passageway" link Room5}, @{"East" link
Room8}, @{"Up" link Room11}

@endnode

@node Room10

@title "The Boudoir"
```

@{"Down" link Room8}, @{"Secret Passageway" link Death}

@endnode

@node Room11

@title "The Bullion Room"

Hurrah! You have found the gold! You are now a multi-millionaire and can retire to the West Indies.

Return to @{"Start" link MAIN}

@endnode

@node Death

@title "Sudden yet Painful Death"

Aaaagh! You have died in one of the more unpleasant manners available.

@{"Try Again" link MAIN}

@endnode

5

**The RAD disk is the Ram Disk with a difference –
it survives a soft reboot. You can also use it for
quick disk copying as this chapter shows...**

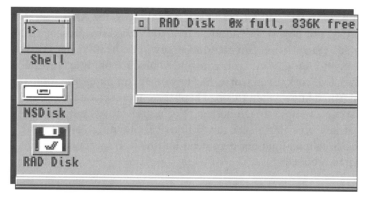

*U*ntil now we have used the Ram Disk to a considerable
extent. One of the easiest and quickest ways to copy
information from one disk to another is to copy it all
into the Ram Disk first.

If you have an extra floppy disk drive or a hard disk unit then
you may be quite happy using this instead for most purposes
but even so there are many occasions when using a Ram Disk
is preferable. Copying files from floppy disk is a slow process –
and why does the disk drive have to make such a pained noise
all the time? If you are using a program which demands the
continual reading of different pieces of information from disk
then you'll soon get pretty fed up of all that screeching and
clanking. The situation isn't anything like as bad for hard disk
drive owners but it is always a useful policy to avoid loading
everything onto the hard drive. Otherwise the device that you
bought thinking you'd never need all that storage space will
rapidly become full.

When you have just bought your A1200 the thought of spending yet more money on an additional disk drive or, even more pricey, a hard disk unit is enough to make the strongest blanch. Using the Ram Disk isn't just the poor man's salvation then but is a handy way of speeding up your computing.

The trouble with the Ram Disk is that it's not very robust. Periodically you need to perform a soft-boot (<Ctrl><Amiga><Amiga>) on the A1200. This can be for many reasons. Some preference settings are only effective after a soft-boot for example. Whatever the reason, the danger of a soft-boot is all too obvious – everything in the Ram Disk is lost. This may not be a severe annoyance if you've had the presence of mind to save anything you needed elsewhere before pressing <Ctrl><Amiga><Amiga> but you can find yourself looking at several hours of wasted work. Even worse, like any other computer, the Amiga can *crash*. You'll know when this has happened because you find yourself confronted with a frozen screen. No mouse movement, button pushing or key pressing makes any difference. Shouting at the computer doesn't help and neither does head-butting it. It has crashed and you'll have to reboot.

Hard and Fast

As ever there is an alternative and on the A1200 it comes in the shape of the RAD disk (RAD:). This is a device which allows you to pretend that part of the Amiga's RAM is a storage device just like a floppy device. And, just like a floppy disk, the RAD disk retains its information after a soft boot. What it won't do, though, is to survive the machine being switched off.

Everything has its price and the cost of the RAD: disk is that it can only be of a fixed capacity. Open the Ram Disk and the legend across the top reads: "Ram Disk 100% full, 0k free, 28k in use". Copy any file across to it and it immediately expands to accommodate it. Delete that file and the Ram Disk shrinks down to its previous capacity. Sure, it does use up some of the machine's precious memory but only as much as is absolutely necessary.

The RAD disk is less flexible. It has to be configured for use just like any other device. Once its dimensions are set they cannot be altered without starting over so you need to know how large a RAD disk you want before you set off.

RAD is to be found in the DOSDrivers directory on the Storage disk. To use it, it needs to be dragged across to the DOSDrivers directory – itself a subdirectory of the Devices directory – on the Workbench disk. One soft boot later and it is ready for use. Removal is the reverse of this process but with one proviso: deleting it from the DOSDrivers directory and a soft reboot is not sufficient because the RAD disk survives a soft reboot! However, on future occasions when the A1200 is switched on the RAD disk will no longer be there.

Once you have placed the RAD device in the DOSDrivers directory you may wish to make some adjustments to the device before using it. To do so you need to read the "mountlist" associated with the device. This can be done by entering the command:

ED DF0:DEVS/DOSDRIVERS/RAD

into the Shell or at the "Execute Command..." option. The following information will be revealed:

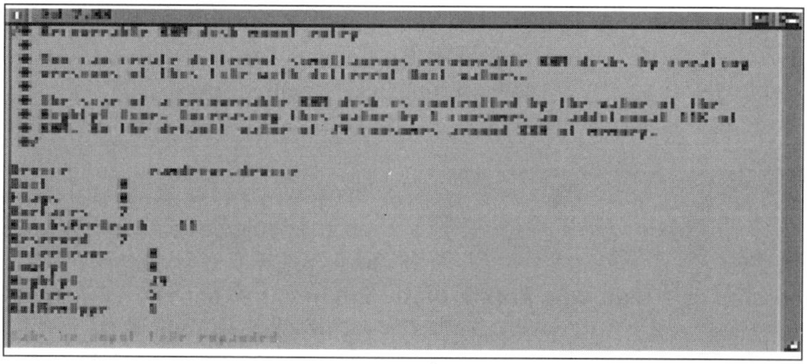

Figure 5.1. The RAD disk Mount file.

There's all sorts of information hidden away here but the only piece that concerns us right now is the "HighCyl" value. This dictates the eventual size of the RAD disk by the formula:

RAD size = (HighCyl value + 1) * 11k

So if the value is 79, then 11K*80 = 880K which is the default setting.

The second important statistic to note is the Unit value. This is important to alter if you wish to create extra RAD disks.

To create a second RAD disk simply make a copy of the first in the DOSDrivers directory. Then alter its "Unit" value in the mountlist to 1 (or to 2 if it's a third RAD disk you are adding, and so on). While the mountlist is open you can also adjust any subsequent RAD disk's size via the HighCyl value while you are at it. What you can't do is to alter the size of any RAD disk while it is in use – even after a soft reboot. The changes will only be made when the machine is switched on.

However, a RAD disk can be removed during normal computer use by using the REMRAD (REMove RAD) command:

REMRAD RAD_1:

or just:

REMRAD

if you are using just the one RAD disk. Normally any changes made to a RAD disk will not be executed after a soft reset. However, the use of REMRAD is one way round this. Alter a RAD disk's mountlist accordingly and save it. Then (REMRAD) remove that RAD disk. Now perform a soft-reset. As the RAD disk is being created anew the latest settings in the mountlist will become active. One final word of warning. The REMRAD command is quite powerful. If you use it indiscriminately to remove a RAD disk which contains precious files, too bad – there's no way of retrieving them. To remove a RAD disk permanently, simply delete the RAD file from the DOSDrivers directory.

RAD Diskcopy

The reason why the RAD disk takes on such a large size by default is because 880K just so happens to be the size of a standard floppy disk. This means that the DISKCOPY command can be used with RAD. Open the Shell and type in:

DISKCOPY DF0: RAD:

After the usual checks to make sure that you have the correct disk in the drive, the A1200 will tick away quite happily until it has made a RAM-based replica of whatever disk you wish. Now placing any disk into the disk drive and reversing the process will produce copies of the disk.

At first this doesn't appear to hold any extra advantages over copying the complete list of disk files into RAM and then across to a new disk but the important part of RAD is that it is actually formatted like a disk. Thus, if you are copying a disk onto an unformatted disk this saves quite a bit of time. Should you be making multiple copies of a disk for whatever reason then the savings will increase accordingly.

Insider Guide #8: Mounting a RAD disk.

A RAD disk can be created from within the Shell using the straight-forward MOUNT RAD: *command. However, for a device to* MOUNT *successfully it must be already available to Workbench. Hard disk users will be quite happy with the above command but for single floppy drive owners who want to use RAD on an occasional basis without recourse to disk juggling there is another solution.*

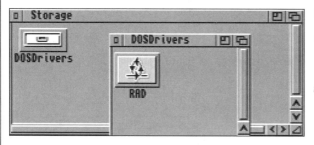

Use the New Directory option from the Workbench and create two drawers on the Workbench disk called "Storage" and "Storage/DOSDrivers". *Copy the RAD disk driver from the Storage:Devices/DOSDrivers directory into this directory and now a RAD disk is available without being automatically produced every time you boot up.*

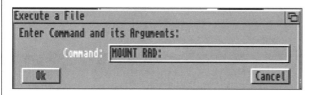

Even if you have two disk drives it could save you hassle when making multiple copies.

You now have enough knowledge to write a simple AmigaDOS program which can DISKCOPY to more than one disk drive and display messages informing the user where it is up to in the process. You're still left with the manual task of loading the disks into the drive but you can get on with something else while you wait. After all, one of the main attractions of computers is their ability to automate repetitive tasks.

Create impressive looking documents using a text editor and the fonts available on the A1200...

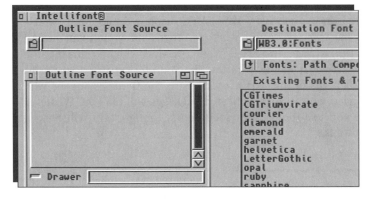

*W*hy do people buy computers in the first place? There are many reasons but at or near the top of the list for just about everyone who uses a computer is the ability to use it for writing with. Typewriters are dead; long live the wordprocessor.

Depending on what you want from this sort of software you can spend anything from a few pounds up to several hundred. At the top level a wordprocessor will check your spelling, analyse your writing style for grammatic deficiencies, number your pages for you and even allow you to incorporate illustrations and tables. But even the cheapest offering from the public domain will produce documents of a high enough quality with which to write letters to your bank manager. The factor which has the greatest bearing on the quality of the end product is not the software you use to write with, but the type of printer used at the end of the process. (See Chapter 12 *Print Out.*)

Home Publishing

The next step up from a wordprocessor is a desktop publishing (DTP) package. There is no clear distinction between the two as the most expensive wordprocessors are often very similar in capabilities.

The main aim in DTP is to produce attractive page layouts for newspapers, magazines, flyers and the like but they can also be used for wordprocessing functions.

The emphasis in DTP is on the visual appearance of a document and for this reason many boast a WYSIWYG display. Pronounced "wizzywig" this has to be one of the worst acronyms known to mankind. All it stands for is "What You See Is What You Get" which means that the image on-screen is identical to the one you will get when you print out. The benefits of this sort of system are enormous as anyone who has struggled with less sophisticated packages will tell you. Whatever software you use for writing documents, though, you will need a choice of fonts.

Type and Fonts

A typeface is the alphabet of letters and associated symbols designed to one particular style. Thus the text in this chapter is written using the *New Aster* typeface, the Insider Guide captions use *Lucida Italic* and the headings for the chapters are written in *Helvetica Light*. If you look closely at a specific letter, you can see how it is drawn differently in the various typefaces.

There are two main forms of typeface – *Serif* and *San Serif*. A Serif typeface has little appendages to the arms of each letter and will often use varying thicknesses in the strokes that make up each letter. San Serif fonts, in contrast, are blockier and without such frippery.

Apart from these two categories you can even buy typefaces designed to look like Gothic lettering, Egyptian hieroglyphics, ink splashes, furry animals and god knows what else. If you want it, shop around and you'll find it.

San Serif and Serif typefaces will be used for most purposes, though, and the next step is determining which size you want. This is where the word "font" comes in. A typeface is the full family of sizes whereas a font refers to one specific size of that typeface. "Helvetica" is a typeface, "Helvetica Bold Ultra Condensed, 16 point" a font.

Insider Guide #9: Bitmap and outline fonts.

An outline font is drawn using mathematical formulae. It is chracterised by having smooth edges throughout no matter at what size it is displayed. This is because the formulae are resolution independent and work at any magnification.

A bitmap font is not resolution independent. It is normally designed to work at one specific size. If the font is enlarged then the font displays jagged edges which distracts from the apperance of the font and can make it very difficult to read.

Both these letter As were set in Times!

Bitmap or Outline

A more technical but equally important distinction is that between *bitmapped* and *outline* fonts. The two terms describe the ways in which the fonts are displayed either on screen or when printed out.

An outline font uses a series of mathematical equations to describe the outline of each individual letter. For a complete alphabet of letters in both upper and lower cases, numbers 0 to 9 plus all the assorted symbols that's a lot of equations. However, once you have, say, the letter "S" described in such a manner it is simplicity itself to specify any point size you care for down to as many decimal places as makes no difference. In addition the font can be expanded in one direction only – horizontal or vertical – without losing any clarity.

Bit-mapped fonts are composed from a number of blocks. As such the file needed to store the details on a given point size of font is considerably smaller in size. But, a new set of files is needed for each additional font size that you want to use. If a bitmapped font is scaled up or down then it appears slightly distorted as a result. Bear this in mind when using bit-mapped fonts. If you wish to use a new size font then pick one which is exactly twice (or three times etc) the size of an existing bitmap image.

Choosing Fonts

Look at how books and magazines use their fonts. Select a design that appeals to you and use it as your starting point. Typically a Serif font like Times is used for the main text and a bold, sans serif text like `Courier` or **Helvetica** for the captions.

Try and restrict the number of fonts you use within a design as otherwise it quickly looks terrible. Don't use *fancy fonts* like Gothic for text as it is largely illegible. If you are wanting to create a historic feel to a document then try using a large Gothic drop capital to start with followed by a serif font for the text.

Intellifont

The Intellifont utility is to be found in the System directory on the Extras disk and can be used to install outline fonts and to convert them into bit-mapped form. The advantage of this is that, if you know in advance, what size of fonts you need for a particular application then the bitmapped versions will take up far less room in memory than having the entire outline structure. The second advantage is that much software is, quite simply, incapable of loading outline fonts!

One feature of Intellifont is its "On-Line Help" facility. Double-click on the Intellifont icon and an application window is launched. Now press the Amiga <Help> key and a screen panel provides information about various aspects of the application's use. Click elsewhere within the window and an explanatory note about each particular function is revealed. Whether you find this sort of On-Line Help useful or not is a matter of taste. Many commercial programs offer this kind of facility but, for my money, I'd rather have a better manual.

Installing Outlines

You will need the Workbench disk, the Extras disk, your Fonts disk and the source disk for the outline fonts you wish to install. With a single disk drive Amiga and no hard disk this is going to call for some serious disk juggling so plan in advance exactly how you are going to accomplish this. One way is to create a RAD disk of about 900k and then copy the Workbench disk into it:

COPY FROM DF0: TO RAD: ALL

Then copy the Intellifont utility into the System directory of this disk and you should still be left with enough space to store any new fonts. Perform a soft reboot and the only disks you will need to swap will be the Fonts disk and the source disk for your new outline fonts.

The Intellifont opening screen is divided into two. The left half is concerned with where you are getting your outline fonts from and the right half with where you wish to install them. Click in the "Outline Font Source" window and type in the disk title of your outline fonts source eg DF0:OUTLINES. Or you can click on the gadget to the left of this and work your way through the "Volumes" and "Drawers" options in a similar fashion as you would use to load a file into MultiView.

The "Source Typefaces" window will now display those outlines fonts it has been directed towards. Click on a font name in this window and then on the "Install Marked Typefaces" button. The font should now be displayed in the righthand window as one of the "Existing Fonts & Typefaces".

Modifying Outlines

Any outline font can be used to create corresponding bitmapped images. The righthand display of the Intellifont window lists all those fonts that are available. Clicking on the "Modify Existing Typefaces..." button reveals yet another window. Here a list is displayed of all the outline typefaces that can be modified. Click on one of these and a list of all the font sizes currently available are shown on the righthand side. If you want to add to these then just type in the number(s) that you want in the "Size" window and click on "Add Size".

To create a bitmap font of any size, first specify the size you want, add it to the "Size and Bitmap" list where it will appear as, for example, "12bitmap" and then click on the "Perform Changes" button. You should now find that the Fonts drawer has been added to.

Variable Change

By default any application that – like Intellifont – lists font sizes in its menus or options will use 15, 30, 45, 60 and 75 point sizes. If you commonly use other point sizes – which you probably do – then you will want to specify a different set of figures. If, for example you are wordprocessing then the text size will be around 9 to 12 point with slightly larger sizes used for headings and so on. This text in this book, for example, is in 10 point size. Seventy-five points, on the other hand, produces lettering slightly more than an inch high which won't be much use. Conversely if you are creating titles for videos then that may be exactly what you need.

Whichever it is to be, the process for altering the default set-ups is simple. Open ED (or any other ASCII text editor) and type in the point sizes that you want. Separate each point size by either a comma or a <Return> – Intellifont is flexible enough to cope with them both. Call this file "Intellifont" and save it in the Extras3.0:Prefs/Env-Archive/Sys directory (or its equivalent on a hard disk of SYS:Prefs/Env-Archive/Sys).

Diskfont Variables

One effect of using different screen modes is that they can adversely affect the shape and hence legibility of fonts you are using. Although modes such as PAL Super-High Res can provide an apparently larger Workbench to use this is no use if you can't read the Workbench menus or icon names. You can control this by adjusting the aspect ratio (the ratio of its width to its height) of a font by playing around with the Diskfont environmental variable.

Create an ED file called:

EXTRAS3.0:PREFS/ENV-ARCHIVE/SYS/DISKFONT

or

SYS:PREFS/ENV-ARCHIVE/SYS/DISKFONT

and in it store the X to Y ratio of the font you wish to produce, in the following format:

XDPI 100 YDPI 50

Now, every time a new bitmap font is created it will be created in the ratio stored in the DISKFONT file. The ratio of XDPI 100 YDPI 50 just so happens to be a means of doubling the width of a screen font. Ideal for using in the higher resolution modes.

Insider Guide #10: Creating a bitmap font.

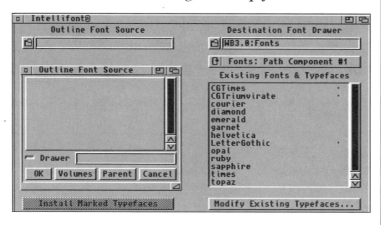

To create a bitmap font first specify the size you require in the "Size"
window. Then click on the "Create Bitmap" button.

Nothing you do in this window has any permanent effect until you
press the "Perform Changes" button so you need have no fears about
making mistakes as you go along. This button in turn produces its
own Intellifont Warning window, listing the changes you have specified and asking for confirmation.

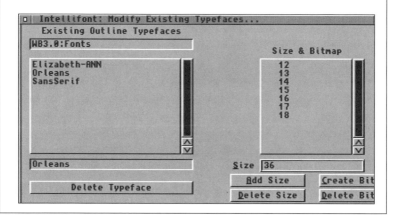

7

Files on the Amiga have *flags* associated with them. These can be used to prevent the accidental erasure of files and to provide a means of checking which files have been archived...

```
┌─────────────────────────────────────────────────────┐
│ □  Ram Disk:                                         │
│                          BOGUS (Project)      Script │
│    Blocks: 12                                Archived │
│     Bytes: 11970            ┌──────┐         Readable │
│                             │ △ ☰  │         Writable │
│     Stack: │4096 │          └──────┘       Executable │
│                                             Deletable │
│ Last Changed: 02-Sep-92 15:18:31                      │
│       Comment: │THIS IS MY COMMENT                   │
│  Default Tool: │                                     │
│                                                       │
└─────────────────────────────────────────────────────┘
```

*Y*ou should by now be familiar with the knack of protecting disks from accidental erasure. All floppy disks have a small movable plastic tab in one corner which can be positioned either to reveal a small hole or to cover it over. With the hole revealed all the information on disk is protected – in computer jargon we say it is *write-protected*. The A1200 can quite easily copy data from such a disk but cannot save any data to it.

In normal usage disks such as the Workbench disk and the Extras disk should be write-protected as a matter of course. The information they hold is vital in the day to day use of the A1200 but, once you have decided on the innumerable options concerning the look and feel of the Workbench, there should be no need to save anything to them. So keep them write-protected simply to prevent overwriting just by mistake.

Fly the Flags!

Permanent write-protection is all very well for some disks but with most others we want to be able to read and write data at will and still not run the risk of deleting valued files. It can, of course, be done and done easily.

Every file on every disk has, associated with it, a number of what are called *flags*. Put the Workbench disk in the drive and open the System directory. Open the Shell by double-clicking and, when prompted, type in:

LIST

There then follows a list of files and directories. The directories are denoted by the letters "dir" and files can be recognised by a figure which is their size in bytes.

After this comes four dashes, the letters "rw-d" a date and a time. The dashes and letters are the file's flags.

```
□  AmigaShell
New Shell process 4
4.WB3.0:> RAM:
4.Ram Disk:> LIST
ENV                          Dir ----rwed Today      15:00:47
Clipboards                   Dir ----rwed Today      15:00:33
T                            Dir ----rwed Today      15:00:49
3 directories - 6 blocks used
4.Ram Disk:>
```

Figure 7.1. AmigaDOS flags.

The meaning of a file's name, its size and the date and time are all pretty obvious, but what does ----rw-d mean? It tells us that the file in question is readable (r), writeable (w), and deletable (d). Whenever a file is created these flags are automatically set by default.

To demonstrate how these work it is probably best to create a new file from scratch otherwise, if something should happen to the files on your Workbench disk, you're not going to be too happy.

With the Shell window open type in:

RAM:

to change the current directory and then create a worthless ED file simply by typing in:

ED BOGUS

This brings up an ED window. Type in:

ECHO "This file is throwaway"

or some such nonsense and then save the file by pressing <ESC> and then <X>. Now type in:

LIST BOGUS

and something similar to the following will be displayed:

BOGUS   31 ——rw-d   Today   12:34:56

A file by the name of "BOGUS" has been created. It is 31 bytes in length, it is readable, writeable and deletable and was created today at about twenty-five to One. To protect the file "BOGUS" from deletion type in:

PROTECT BOGUS -D

Which removes the d (deletable) flag. Type in:

LIST BOGUS

one more time and the line looks like this:

BOGUS 31 ——rw—   Today 12:34:56

Now if we try and delete our BOGUS file we find that it is no longer possible:

DELETE BOGUS

**BOGUS Not deleted: object is protected from dele-
tion**

Which is of course exactly what we want. And this can be used to protect any file from being accidentally erased. To make the file deletable once more the opposite command can be used:

PROTECT BOGUS +D

and now if we use the:

DELETE BOGUS

command, it works and we receive the message:

BOGUS Deleted

More Flags

AmigaDOS reveals several flags for each file. There are seven flags in total which can be set altogether: s, p, a, w, r, e and d. These initial letters stand for script, pure, archived, writeable, readable, executable and deletable.

The idea behind the readable flag is that the file is safe from the casual gaze of prying eyes. With the readable flag switched off we might reasonably expect that it is no longer possible to read the file. Not so! Someone, somewhere has dropped a clanger and the readable flag doesn't appear to do anything. Not to worry, though, because as a means of keeping a file secret it wasn't exactly foolproof. It also provides an interesting lesson for those new to computing. With the vast amounts of software around and the number of combinations and permutations of commands available it's surprising that bugs like this don't crop up more often. It's always worth remembering, if something does go wrong with the software and hardware that you are using, that it might not be your fault.

The write flag switched off still lets us look at the information within a file but prevents the saving of any alterations. As an exercise it is worth playing round with a similar file to the BOGUS one created in the example above as one or two curiosities emerge.

If we use the example as above and create a BOGUS file, the writeable protection seems to make no difference. We can create a file, protect it with the "-w" setting, make changes to it and save it; so much for the so-called write-protection. Why does this happen? It's because different programs save their files in different ways. Some, like ED, don't save any changes made to the old file but instead they go through the entire saving process all over again, overwriting any existing file of the same name. It is as well to find out, before you start relying on file protection of this manner, exactly how the software you are using treats its files.

The Script Flag

The "s" flag tells AmigaDOS that the file is an AmigaDOS script file. The "BOGUS" file we created previously was a script file but if we type in:

    BOGUS

as a command the reply is:

    BOGUS: file is not executable

But, by switching the s flag on and typing in BOGUS the script can be executed:

```
PROTECT BOGUS +S
BOGUS
This file is throwaway
```

Pure Flags

The "p" flag stands for Pure. This is somewhat beyond the realm of this tome but any file that is capable of being made resident is called "pure" and can bear the "p" flag. However, simply attaching "p" to a script is not sufficient to render it pure.

To complete the picture, the "e" flag controls whether a command is executable or not. For example the command:

```
PROTECT C:COPY -E
```

prevents the COPY command from being used. I can't think of too many uses for it at this stage. Incidentally I advise against the use of commands such as:

```
PROTECT LIST -E
```

or

```
PROTECT PROTECT -E
```

Workbench Flags

There are two ways in which file flags can be changed from the Workbench. The first method is by using the "Execute Command…" option in the Workbench Menu. This allows for one-line commands to be entered without having to load up Shell. So for example the command:

```
PROTECT DF0:BOOK/CHAPTER#? -D
```

will secure all the files that start with the letters "chapter" contained in the "Book" directory of the disk in drive DF0: against deletion.

Files can also be accessed from the Workbench via the "Information" option in the Icons menu. The file we were working on – "BOGUS" – is stored in the Ram Disk. Open the Ram Disk by double-clicking on its icon and then select the "Show >> All Files" option from the Window menu.

The RAM: directory now displays three directories: ENV, T and Clipboards, and one file: BOGUS. Information about any of these can be read and altered by selecting the file and then choosing the Information option from the Icons menu. This pops up a window with roughly the same information as we had about BOGUS in the Shell but presented in a much more user-friendly fashion.

The file flags (other than pure) are accessed via a series of *toggle switches* down the righthand side of the window with a tick (or check) indicating that that flag is set. It is worth playing around with these and looking to see what happens. With the BOGUS file I have been playing around with it tells me that the file is a Project and that it is readable, writeable and deletable.

By clicking on the "Script" and "Executable" options and then clicking "Save" AmigaDOS is told that BOGUS is a script file and that it's ready to go.

Select "Update" from the Window menu and BOGUS is now represented by a hammer head icon – which relates to "Tool" in the information window. Now try double-clicking on the BOGUS icon and see what happens.

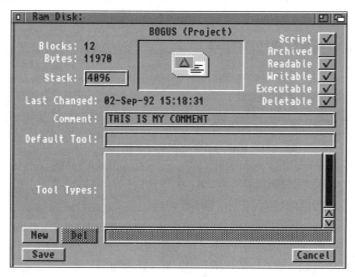

Figure 7.2. The Information window for BOGUS.

One other option in the Information window is the Comment box. Absolutely anything can be written in here and it has no bearing on the physical workings of the file. Should your comment be longer than

---

Insider Guide #11: Protecting a file from deletion.

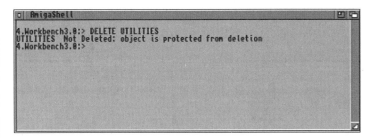

```
AmigaShell
4.Workbench3.0:> DELETE UTILITIES
UTILITIES  Not Deleted: object is protected from deletion
4.Workbench3.0:>
```

Choose a file that you wish to protect from deletion – I have chosen one called "Bogus". LIST the file to see the state of its flags.

LIST RAM:BOGUS

BOGUS   11 ----rwed   Today   12:34:56

1 file – 2 blocks used

Protect the file by turning the "D" flag – deletable – off.

PROTECT RAM:BOGUS -D

Any attempt to delete the file will now fail.

DELETE RAM:BOGUS

FILE PROTECTED FROM DELETION

Note: this cannot protect a file from some accidental erasures such as formatting the disk on which it is stored.

---

the Comment box then the text will scroll to allow a few more characters. This is a very useful way of storing additional information about what the file contains that can't be included in the file name.

Return to the Shell and type in:

LIST RAM:BOGUS

and the usual information is displayed in the manner we have come to expect with the addition of a line of commentary beneath it. As ever this is also accessible from the Shell. We use the FILENOTE command:

FILENOTE BOGUS THIS IS MY COMMENT

LIST BOGUS

BOGUS

THIS IS MY COMMENT

It is worth remembering that although the Workbench and AmigaDOS are quite different from each other in many respects, they do provide access to a lot of common features. With practice you should be able to swap between the two quite happily and get the most out of the machine.

Archiving

The "a" flag denotes that the file is archived. If the concept of an archive to you is the dusty and undisturbed part of a library where no-one ever ventures then you're on the right tracks for understanding a computer archive. All the "a" flag does is show that the file has not been used since the "a" flag was set. If the file is inspected or additional data saved to it then the flag disappears. To demonstrate how this works select a file to play with and set it to archived:

PROTECT FILE PROTECT +A

Using the LIST command will confirm that the flag is now set to "a". Now let's just take a look at the file by using ED:

RUN ED FILE

Yes, that looks fine, close the file once more. Now, if the file is LISTed you will notice that the "a" flag has disappeared.

This may not seem particularly exciting and at first glance appears fairly useless. Where it comes into its own is when backups of large numbers of files are made. This is a regular event for owners of hard disks but there is no reason why all computer users shouldn't save copies of their precious files. After all, you never know when you're going to spill coffee over your stack of disks!

The way an archiving program works is, in principle, very simple. It just keeps a list of all the files on your record and makes a copy of each one. As it does so it switches on the archive flag of each file. The next time you make a back-up the program checks to see which files still have their archive "a" flags. It ignores those that do (because they haven't changed) and just makes copies of those files that have been updated or any file that is totally new.

Bit of a Squash

Compression is a means of making a file smaller in size. It can be done in a variety of ways and with a variety of programs but the principles remain the same. A file compressor searches a file for repetitious chunks and replaces them with a piece of code. This is done in such a way that the decompression program can recognise what has been done and reverse the operation. Imagine a wordprocessed document in which every letter is repeated four times. The compression utility comes along, spots this anomaly, removes the repeats and leaves a message for the decompression utility about what it has done. Voila – a file one quarter of its previous size! OK, so the example is a little fanciful to say the least but that's the rough idea. Another point worth bearing in mind is that the wordprocessor which was used to create the original file will no longer be able to read it. That's because at the head of every file there is some form of identification to say "This is a wordprocessor file" or whatever. When a file is compressed a message is written in front of this to say: "This is a compressed file".

If you buy one of the Amiga magazines with a disk or two strapped to the cover then you will invariably find that the disks contain compressed data. It's a great way for the publishers to maximise the amount of material they can put out with each issue and give tremendous value for money. It does mean, however, that before you can use whatever is on the disks you have to decompress the data first. Luckily the decompression utility is also provided and in such a way that you hardly need know it's there. As a general rule all you have to do is double-click on the icon of the program you wish to use and then feed the A1200 with blank preformatted disks as it directs. At the end of the procedure you will find that you now have a decompressed version of the cover disks saved onto several disks.

A compression utility is invariably made available in two parts: the one that compresses the data and the one that decompresses it. The decompression part is freely available to anyone who wants it – the compression part is the one that you have to pay for. If all you ever want to do is expand the data on magazine or PD disks then this needn't worry you. If you want to compress files of your own then you'll need a compressor.

The advantage of compression is not just a saving in terms of the cost of disks but also in actually being able to save data. A 1Mb file can't normally be saved onto an 800K floppy disk but it can if it has been compressed!

The downside to compression/decompression is that it takes time. You don't want to have to decompress every single file every time you want to make the smallest alteration only to have to recompress afterwards; it would take far too long. But, for data that you have saved in your archives, for example, it could be just the ticket.

8

Deleting a file on the Amiga isn't as final as may at first appear. There's still the chance of being able to rescue lost data – and not just by you!

Learn how to make the Great Escape by careful planning and the employment of disk utilities.

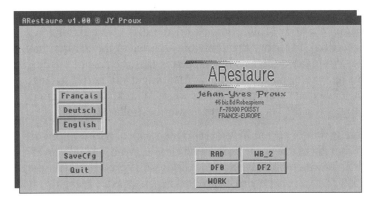

hen you are using commands such as DISKCOPY the A1200 provides a variety of so-called "safety net" instructions such as:

    Insert disk to copy from (SOURCE disk) in
    device RAD

    Insert disk to copy to (DESTINATION disk)
    in device DF0

    Press RETURN to begin copying or CTRL-C to
    abort:

This is all well and good but what happens if you follow the instructions to the letter and only realise once you have started copying or formatting or whatever instruction it is that you are carrying out, that you have the wrong disk in the disk drive? Disaster!

All those hours of work ruined, your best-selling novel erased for good. The quick answer is that you should be more careful. The disk with your best-selling novel on should be clearly labelled "Best-Selling Novel" and you should make regular back-ups. But, we're only human and mistakes do occur.

So imagine the situation where you have started writing over some valuable files. The first thing to do is to stop the process. Hold down the <Ctrl> key and press <C>. This stops the formatting or disk copying process. The message "***Break" now appears. A lot now depends on how soon you managed to stop the process. For example if you are formatting a disk the line above "***Break" will read something like:

```
Verifying cylinder 19, 60 to go
```

Which means that out of 80 *cylinders* on the disk one quarter have been over-written. In theory then only one-quarter of the damage has been done. What can quite feasibly happen is that the part of the disk which you have reformatted or over-written might not be those parts where you have done your most recent work. Who knows – you may not have to rewrite the latest chapters of your bestseller after all!

The trouble is that once you have over-written part of a disk, trying to find out what hasn't been destroyed isn't easy. Put a partially over-written disk into the disk drive and the disk icon is produced with the title "DF0:????". In other words the Workbench doesn't recognise it and is refusing to read it. But the information, some information, is still there and it must be possible to read it. What is needed is a specific program to do the job.

No, Not Me

After reading the above example you may be thinking. "I'm too careful, it couldn't happen to me". You may well be right, some of us are more organised than others but there can be few computer users who have not accidentally erased a file only to realise that they have erased the wrong one. Another disaster! But, once again, all is not lost. You may think that once you have erased some data then that's it, end of story, goodbye to several hours work; not so.

Compare the amount of time it takes to copy a large file to disk with the amount of time taken to delete it. The larger the file the longer it takes to copy but deletion is pretty instantaneous, how come?

When you put a disk into the A1200 it doesn't read the entire disk – that would take far too long – instead it just looks for the sector on the disk where it knows the disk's name will be stored, reads that part and displays the information. Similarly when you double-click on the disk icon to display the disk contents it just reads that sector of the disk where the information about files is kept. If a file is stored on disk but doesn't have this information attached then it will appear not to exist.

However, a file's existence and name isn't the only information that is stored in this sector of the disk. The other vital part is information about where the file is located. This is important not only to help find the file but also to prevent it from being over-written by another one.

When a file is deleted the only part that actually disappears is the part that states it exists and claims some space for it. All the rest of the information remains although it is now in danger of being over-written by any subsequent files that might be saved on that disk. Accidentally wipe out a file and there is no cause for alarm – if you realise quickly enough what you have done, it may be recoverable.

Rescue Stations

Fortunately the process of reading a disk and displaying everything that can be found on it is not particularly difficult for the competent A1200 programmer and there are many programs around – both commercially and in the public domain – which can rescue data after a disk has been partially formatted or after a file has been deleted.

Without getting too bogged down in the details, the program will usually require a source disk and a destination for anything it finds on it. The source disk will be the one where the damage has been done and any data rescued can be relayed to the Ram Disk for example.

Whilst on the subject of Ram Disks it is worth noting that anything deleted from a Ram Disk is unrecoverable even if the machine has been kept switched on.

File Paranoia

Deleting a file, as we have seen, is a simple process of removing that part of it which tells the A1200's operating system of its existence. Anyone can come along, armed with the appropriate piece of software, and inspect disks to find out what was stored there before. So what? Most of the time this is of absolutely no importance whatsoever. Who cares if a Peeping Tom sees the first aborted draft of one of my letters? If you never have anything to hide then skip this section but if you work for military intelligence or you're paranoid then you will want to know how to make sure that no remnants of a file are left behind, The quickest way of doing this is to save the files that you do want from the device and then *quick format* that device.

Disk Storage

Electronic storage on disk is like any other filing system so it can become cluttered. The more cluttered a filing system is the longer it takes to find what you are looking for and this can happen with computers as much as it can with the more conventional paper-hungry office.

Imagine you have a floppy disk packed with lots of tiny files. Each file is stored in its own separate sector and can be found quite rapidly. After a while you have no need for half of them so you delete them. The title bar on the Workbench screen now informs you that the disk is, say 50% full and has 440K of free storage space. Just enough room, in fact, for a large picture file that you want to save. What happens is that, in saving the data for the picture file, the A1200 chops up the file into little segments to fit into all the available spaces created by removing the smaller wordprocessor files. As these spaces are scattered randomly across the disk, actually storing all the information for the file takes longer.

Now imagine that you have no need for the remaining tiny files and so you delete them and replace them with another large picture file. The net result is two, large picture files horribly interwoven.

OK so it's a rather contrived example but it's only a more extreme version of what is happening all the time. You have two files stored on disk with their data seemingly entwined. Instead of File A occupying sectors 0-39 and File B occupying sectors 40-79, say, File A is to be found on sectors 1, 3, 6, 7, 11 etc and File B on sectors 2, 4, 5, 8 etc. If you think this is bad enough, imagine the fun that can be had with storing information on a hard disk! Thousands of files all chopped up with bits of them all over the place.

There is, of course, no quick way round the problem. Using a computer on a regular basis means the creation and deletion of an endless number of files.

So what can be done about it? Answer: take one freshly formatted disk and copy files A and B to it. The A1200 by default stores information

Insider Guide #12: Rescuing a file using ARestaure.

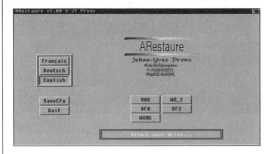

ARestaure is a public domain utility available on the NextSteps disk and elsewhere. Its use is simplicity itself. To demonstrate I have copied the Startup-Sequence file – as "s-s" – to a freshly formatted disk and then deleted it.

Double-click on the AResature icon and the opening screen offers you a choice of three languages and a list of those drives currently available. In my case they are DF0: DF2: Work: WB_2 and RAD.

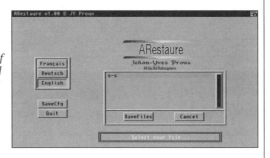

The file I wish to rescue is on DF2: so click on that icon. The disk in that drive is then searched and a list of recovered files produced, just "s-s" in this case.

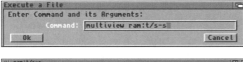

Select the files to be restored and they are transferred to the T: directory on the RAM Disk. Use MultiView to read a text file to see how much has been saved.

Note: If you realise immediately after deleting it that you have made a mistake then a file is normally recoverble.

Files are not recoverable from the Ram Disk.

in an ordered and logical manner and the two files will be positioned aongside each other in a non-segmented fashion. The best thing to do with the old disk is to use Quick Format on it which will erase the data from the deleted files.

9

What happens when the A1200 is switched on, why does it take so long and how can it be improved? Read on...

```
□ | s:startup-sequence
; $VER: startup-sequence 39.9 (9.8.92)

; C:SetPatch QUIET
C:Version >NIL:
C:AddBuffers >NIL: DF0: 15
FailAt 21

C:MakeDir RAM:T RAM:Clipboards RAM:ENV RAM:ENV/Sys
C:Copy >NIL: ENVARC: RAM:ENV ALL NOREQ

Resident >NIL: C:Assign PURE
Resident >NIL: C:Execute PURE

Assign >NIL: ENV: RAM:ENV
Assign >NIL: T: RAM:T
Assign >NIL: CLIPS: RAM:Clipboards
Assign >NIL: REXX: S:
Assign >NIL: PRINTERS: DEVS:Printers
Assign >NIL: KEYMAPS: DEVS:Keymaps
Assign >NIL: LOCALE: SYS:Locale
Assign >NIL: LIBS: SYS:Classes ADD
Assign >NIL: HELP: LOCALE:Help DEFER
--- More (44%) ---
```

S witch on your A1200. There, on the screen, is an animation of a disk inserting itself into the disk drive. The machine is asking you to insert a disk into its floppy disk drive so it can get on with the serious business of running programs.

But the A1200 doesn't want just any old disk in the drive, it wants a "boot" disk. In the early days with your machine this is most likely to be the Workbench disk although many applications come on boot disks of their own – games in particular.

The next stage is the long wait while the A1200 works its way through the disk and loads the appropriate software in a manner that suits the user.

Once the boot disk is inserted into the floppy disk drive the A1200 checks it to make sure that the disk is indeed a boot disk. Once happy with that it looks to see if the boot disk contains a startup file. If it does then that file is executed, otherwise a default startup from ROM is used.

Startup Sequence

Below is a list of the startup-sequence commands and a brief explanation of what they are doing. You may, of course, wish to play around with this file to find out how it works but be warned that if you do so and something goes wrong (which is as inevitable as day following night) then you won't be able to load up Workbench. No problem if you are using a copy of your Workbench disk (which in itself should be a copy of a master disk put away for safe-keeping). But, if you're not following even this simple precaution then you're not just asking for trouble; you're on your knees grovelling for it.

1   ; $VER: startup-sequence 39.9 (9.8.92)

A line of information as denoted by the semi-colon (;) prefix. It announces which version of the startup-sequence we are seeing and when it was written.

2   C:SetPatch QUIET

Setpatch is a bug fixer. No-one can get it right all the time and this command addresses those bugs in the Kickstart ROM that Commodore are aware of. The QUIET option, like >NIL:, prevents Setpatch from producing any output.

3   C:Version >NIL:

Reads in the KickStart and Workbench version numbers. Direction to >NIL: is used this time for the simple reason that the VERSION command does not offer a QUIET option.

4   C:AddBuffers >NIL: DF0: 15

The buffer is an area of memory put aside for storing transitory information. So, for example, when a disk is being read one whole buffer's worth of data at a time is read before being passed on to whatever program wants to use it. The units used are in half kilobytes so, in this startup-sequence 7½K of RAM has been put aside to act as a buffer for drive DF0:.

5   FailAt 21

This is something along the lines of "Carry on Regardless". Errors encountered in AmigaDOS tend to halt the process and make the machine wait for further instructions. If the Startup-Sequence behaved like this then it would have a very long wait indeed. As most of what's happening isn't displayed to screen there's no way the user can possibly see what error has occurred. The "FailAt 21" command takes this into account and even if one line of the Startup-Sequence produces an error it instructs the A1200 to carry on with the next line and get to the end of the script no matter what.

```
6  C:MakeDir RAM:T RAM:Clipboards RAM:ENV
   RAM:ENV/Sys
```

Creates the "T", "Clipboards", ENV" and ENV/Sys" directories on the Ram Disk. The T directory is used for storing temporary files, the Clipboard directory for clipboard files, the ENV directory for global environmental variables and the ENV/Sys directory for Prefs settings.

```
7  C:Copy >NIL: ENVARC: RAM:ENV ALL NOREQ
```

Copies preference settings to RAM.

```
8  Resident >NIL: C:Assign PURE

9  Resident >NIL: C:Execute PURE
```

Makes the ASSIGN and EXECUTE commands resident commands. This means that they are stored in RAM rather than kept on the disk. This means that every time one of these commands is needed the A1200 has it ready to hand rather than having to load it off the disk. This speeds up the Startup-Sequence quite considerably.

```
10 Assign >NIL: ENV: RAM:ENV

11 Assign >NIL: T: RAM:T

12 Assign >NIL: CLIPS: RAM:Clipboards

13 Assign >NIL: REXX: S:

14 Assign >NIL: PRINTERS: DEVS:Printers

15 Assign >NIL: KEYMAPS: DEVS:Keymaps

16 Assign >NIL: LOCALE: SYS:Locale

17 Assign >NIL: LIBS: SYS:Classes ADD

18 Assign >NIL: HELP: LOCALE:Help DEFER
```

The ASSIGN command provides a short-hand notation for commonly used locations. When, for example, T: is used in AmigaDOS it is understood that the directory T in the Ram Disk is meant. Similarly when LIBS: is used AmigaDOS looks for the Classes directory on the SYS: disk. (The SYS: disk is whichever disk is being used to boot up the machine. Typically this is the Workbench disk but can mean any boot disk.)

```
19 IF NOT EXISTS SYS:Fonts
```

```
20    Assign FONTS:

21 EndIF
```

By default the machine will look for a FONTS volume whenever fonts are accessed. If there is a SYS:Fonts directory then that's fine (line 19), if not then a directory is assigned (line 20). Line 21 closes this construction.

```
22 BindDrivers
```

Some hardware that can be attached to the A1200 needs the computer to check for its existence, BINDDRIVERS does just that. It is not needed for hard disk drives, monitors, additional floppy drives or just about any recent hardware. In fact the only time it is used is for devices that require a file loading into the "Expansion" directory. It has been included for reasons of backwards compatibility.

```
23 C:Mount >NIL: DEVS:DOSDrivers/~(#?.info)
```

Mounts any RAD disks, MS DOS drivers etc that might be found in the DOSDrivers subdirectory of the Devs directory. Note from the way the command has been written that it executes any files it finds in DOSDrivers directory which don't have the .info suffix. The >NIL: device prevents any output from being displayed.

```
24 IF EXISTS DEVS:Monitors

25    IF EXISTS DEVS:Monitors/VGAOnly

26       DEVS:Monitors/VGAOnly

27    EndIF

28    C:List >NIL:
DEVS:Monitors/~(#?.info|VGAOnly)
TO T:M LFORMAT "DEVS:Monitors/%s"

29    Execute T:M

30    C:Delete >NIL: T:M

31 EndIF
```

This little chunk is looking to find which monitor the A1200 can expect to send its output to. It checks to see if there are any monitor drivers in the DEVS:Monitors directory and makes them into a script file in RAM:T. This is then executed and finally deleted.

```
32 SetEnv Workbench $Workbench

33 SetEnv Kickstart $Kickstart
```

```
34 UnSet Workbench
35 UnSet Kickstart
```

Cop out – I don't want to get onto the subject of global and local environmental variables.

```
36 C:IPrefs
```

Any changes that the user has saved in the default preference settings – screen colours etc – are executed by this command.

```
37 C:ConClip
```

Sets the Clipboard facility up ready for action

```
38 Path >NIL: RAM: C: SYS:Utilities SYS:Rexxc
        SYS:System S: SYS:Prefs SYS:WBStartup
        SYS:Tools SYS:Tools/Commodities
```

Each time an AmigaDOS command is entered the A1200 has to search for that command before it can execute it. These can be stored in a variety of places all of which are listed in this command.

```
39 IF EXISTS S:User-Startup
40    Execute S:User-Startup
41 EndIF
```

If there is a file called "S:User-Startup" then now is the time to execute it. This allows customisations to be made.

```
42 Resident Execute REMOVE
43 Resident Assign REMOVE
```

Reverses the action of lines 8 and 9 as the commands are no longer needed to be Resident. Doing this leaves more RAM available for use.

```
44 C:LoadWB
```

Launches Workbench (surprise, surprise).

```
45 EndCLI >NIL:
```

End of process.

So that's the Startup-Sequence and it gives us some idea as to what files are being used as a matter of routine. There do seem to be quite a number of them.

Fine Tuning

Having looked at the Startup-Sequence file and gained a feel for what it does you may well be tempted into making amendments to it. There are one or two adjustments which can be made straight away. The command BINDDRIVERS can be deleted, for example, if you have no expansions fitted and this will save a little time in the booting process. You can also remove the lines relating to VGAOnly monitors unless you are so equippe. But in general it is best to leave the file as is until you are more adept with AmigaDOS and concentrate instead on additions that can be made.

Additions can be made to the file and the best way to do this is via the User-Startup file. Write a script of that name and store it in the S: directory and it will be executed as part of the boot procedure.

Boot Disks

Any formatted disk can be made into a boot disk simply by placing it in the internal drive and using the command:

    INSTALL DF0:

Even a blank disk can be INSTALLed in this way although it won't do you much good. All that this process does is write a small piece of code onto the disk which informs the A1200 that this is indeed a boot disk. The A1200 then searches for a file called "Startup-Sequence" in the S: directory on that disk. If it doesn't find this then it uses a default from Kickstart which resembles a Shell window but with very few commands to play with.

So, on our boot disk we need the S directory, a file called "Startup-Sequence" and what else? Anything that the Startup-Sequence file expects to find would be helpful. On the Workbench3.0 "Startup-Sequence" this includes the files listed in the table opposite.

There are one or two unexpected files on there: version.library, Clipboard.device and system-configuration for example. Apart from those, the disk is about as pared down to the bone as you can get, there's about 700K free for any other files that you wish to use.

Directory	Subdirectories/Files
Prefs	Presets
	Env-Archive
	Env-Archive/Sys/wbconfig.prefs
Devs	Clipboard.device
	system-configuration
	DataTypes
	DOSDrivers
	Keymaps
	Monitors
	Printers
C	Addbuffers
	Assign
	BindDrivers
	ConClip
	Copy
	Delete
	Execute
	IPrefs
	List
	LoadWB
	MakeDir
	Mount
	SetPatch
	Version
Libs	version.library
S	Startup-Sequence

Table 9.1. Important directories and files for a boot disk.

Incidentally this isn't the method that all commercial software will use. The most crucial part of this whole boot-up procedure has been to load the Workbench. If you want to start booting up non-Workbench disks – as many games do, for example – then I'm afraid your ambition has taken you beyond the scope of this book.

The contents of the Devs subdirectories is up to you. If you want to use, say, a printer then you'll need to load a suitable driver into the Printers subdirectory and the Printer.device file into the Devs directory.

As it is, this boot disk doesn't serve any great purpose. If you remember the whole point of creating it was so we could have a disk specific to one particular purpose. If that purpose was a wordprocessing disk for example, then the wordprocessor needs to be copied across onto this disk. Now would also be a good time to create an extra drawer, perhaps called "Text Files", for storing work in as it progresses.

The stripped down version of the boot disk may also lack certain files that the wordprocessor expects to find. Files that have been omitted from the table but which will be frequently in demand include:

Libs:asl.library

Libs:commodities.library

and, if you can spare the room, you might as well copy the entire Libs directory across. If a file isn't there which your wordprocessor needs when booting up then it will normally complain and a message will be sent to the Workbench screen saying which file wasn't found. This is a less than ideal way of making sure that you have all you need but is effective nonetheless. For example if you try to format a disk with the pared down Workbench disk then the message reads:

Unable to open your tool 'SYS:System/Format'

Not only does this tell you which tool is missing but it also says where it expects to find it. Similarly your wordprocessor may have files of its own that it needs to read to boot up effectively. These won't be on the Workbench disk but will come with the wordprocessor.

Other files can be added as you need them. If you want to use commands like DISKCOPY then they will have to be placed in the appropriate directory or you will be faced with the helpful:

DISKCOPY : Unknown command

DISKCOPY failed returncode 10

Familiarity with AmigaDOS lets you increase the efficiency of your computing. It also provides one or two handy utilities...

```
□ | S:Ed-startup                                              回|
    Commands:
  <Space> ........ Next Page (More)
  <Return> ....... Next Line
  q or ctrl/c .... Quit
  h .............. Help
  /string ........ Search for string (case sensitive)
  .string ........ Search for string (not case sensitive)
  n .............. Find next occurence of string
  CTRL/L ......... Refresh window
  < .............. First Page
  > .............. Last Page
  %N ............. Move N% into file
  b or <BackSpace> Previous Page (Less)
  E .............. Edit using editor set in ENV:EDITOR
```

*H*aving developed a taste for working with typed commands rather than using a mouse and menus it is time to go a little further into the Shell to see some more of AmigaDOS's usefulness. This isn't the whole AmigaDOS story by a long way. Whole books could be written on the subject and, in fact, they have been. If you are intrigued to delve further then two volumes from the *Mastering AmigaDOS 3* series by Mark Smiddy should be on your shelves. See the Bruce Smith Books Appendix for further details.

And There's More

The A1200 is blessed with a wide variety of mechanisms for viewing the contents of files. At the top-end there's MultiView but even simple commands like TYPE and ED can be used to view ASCII text. The next one to have a look at is MORE. It is particularly useful as it is so straightforward to use. At its most basic MORE can be launched from the Shell with a:

MORE filename

type command. The Startup-Sequence file, for example, can be viewed in this manner:

MORE SYS:S/Startup-Sequence

which loads the relevant file into the current Shell window. As the whole file is too large to be viewed at once, the message "more" is displayed at the bottom of the window with an indication of how far through the file has been reached. Press the spacebar and the next chunk can be seen, the backspace key reverting us to the previous view. When the end of the file is reached an "End of File" message is shown. At this point using the spacebar returns to the command line.

The alternative way of viewing a file using MORE is via the RUN command:

RUN MORE SYS:S/Startup-Sequence

This puts the file being viewed into its own display window. Within MORE the spacebar and backspace act as before and if you press <H> (for "Help") you are shown a list of MORE commands.

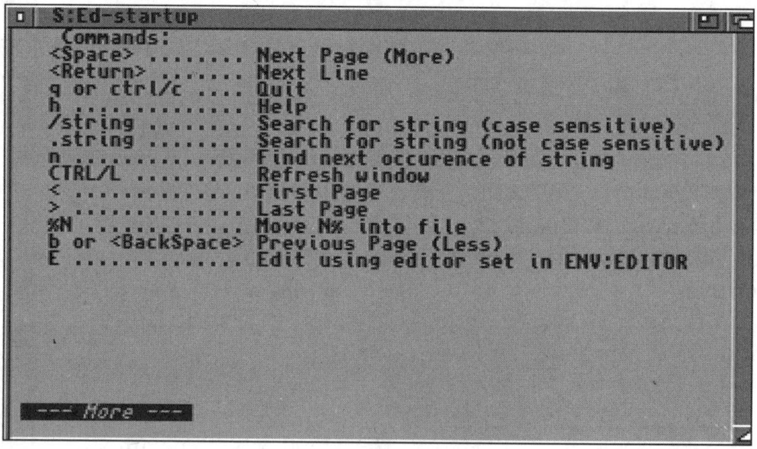

Figure 10.1. Pressing H will list the More commands.

MORE is similar in operation to the ReadMe files that are to be found on so many Public Domain or magazine cover disks. Double-click on one of these and you are provided with notes about the program or programs on offer. Many of these use a simple program which has been specifically written to do just this but you can create your own using the MORE utility. Try it yourself, if you're having trouble see the Insider Guide at the end of this chapter.

PCD

A convenience tool if ever there was one, PCD offers a way of quickly switching between two directories. Using AmigaDOS often involves hopping around between directories, sometimes on different disks. Continually typing in these directory names can be a laborious procedure. There are several ways round this problem, one is to use the ALIAS command, another to use PCD.

Instead of using the CD command to change to a directory that will be used frequently, try using the PCD command. That directory is set up as being one of the two directories that can be toggled between. Study the following:

```
1.Workbench3.0:> PCD SYS:Utilities

1.Workbench3.0:Utilities> PCD
                    Extras3.0:Tools/Commodities

1.Extras3.0:Tools/Commodities> PCD

1.Workbench3.0:Utilities> PCD

1.Extras3.0:Tools/Commodities>
```

The first two lines of this sequence designate the two directories which we wish to hop back and forwards between. Further use of PCD lets us do just that. Much the same effect can be achieved using the ALIAS command:

```
1.Workbench3.0:> ALIAS SU SYS:Utilities

1.Workbench3.0:> ALIAS ETC

Extras3.0:Tools/Commodities

1.Workbench3.0:> ETC

1.Extras3.0:Tools/Commodities> SU

1.Workbench3.0:Utilities>
```

and so on. Take your pick.

Path to Success

As the use of RESIDENT in the AmigaDOS chapter implied, the various AmigaDOS commands tend to be strewn around the place. Some are permanently stored on a ROM chip in the computer memory, others are to be found in the C: directory on the boot disk. FORMAT, however is in the System directory while PCD can be found in the S directory. The question is "How does the A1200 know where to look?"

The answer is through the PATH command. The most commonly used PATH names are set by default as part of the Startup process. These can be read by typing in:

    PATH

which produces the following list:

    Current_directory

    Ram disk

    Workbench3.0:C

    Workbench3.0:Utilities

    Workbench3.0:Rexxc

    Workbench3.0:System

    Workbench3.0:S

    Workbench3.0:Prefs

    Workbench3.0:WBStartup

To add a PATH to these, for example the Tools directory on the Extras disk then try:

    PATH EXTRAS3.0:TOOLS

Now, if you type in:

    RUN CALCULATOR

the A1200 will know exactly what you are on about.

MEmacs

Pronounced Micro-EMACS, the Tools directory on the Extras disk is home to this, yet another, Amiga text editor. Like ED it can be used to create, append and save a text file but unlike ED it also offers a whole host of features which make editing files easier.

MEmacs can be launched either by double-clicking on its icon in the Tools directory or directly from the Shell, with the proviso that the Shell has already been informed of the right PATH.

When launched from the Shell the MEmacs command can be appended with the file name of either an existing file or a new one to be created, for example:

```
MEMACS "RAM:NEW FILE"
```

(Forget the quotation marks and you will find two MEmacs files created "RAM:NEW" and "FILE".) This rather clumsily brings me round to one of MEmacs' features. When the program is run its window occupies the screen and cannot be reduced in size. It can, however, be split into two or more compartments and this can be used either to view two separate files or two sections of the same file. In fact MEmacs has no less than 78 menu options from eight pull-down menus, enough surely for most users' needs.

With that wealth of options there's no way I'm going to detail them all here but suffice it to say that files can be saved and loaded via the menu system which also contains commands to cut and paste, delete and search. These can also be performed via hot key combinations which are listed on the menus themselves. Of particular use is the ability to point with the mouse to the place in the text where you wish to edit rather than having to position the cursor rather laboriously with the arrow keys. Being more complex MEmacs takes a while to get used to but in the long run will be worth the effort.

Search me, Guv

SEARCH is a fast and convenient way of hunting through a file for a "string" of letters and/or numbers.

Its use is predictably easy:

```
SEARCH FILE STRING
```

In this example the file "FILE" is scoured for any instances of the string "STRING". If any are found they are spooled out with the line number and line where they were found. Thus:

```
SEARCH SYS:S/STARTUP-SEQUENCE EXE
```

produces the following output:

```
12 Resident >NIL: C:Execute PURE

37 Execute T:M

53 Execute S:User-Startup

56 Resident Execute REMOVE
```

Each line contains in it somewhere the letters e-x-e. Use the NONUM option at the end of the command and the numbers are omitted from the output.

Sort Of

If you're using your machine for keeping records of any kind then you will doubtless need some or all of them sorted into alphabetical order at one time or another. The SORT command can be used to processe the contents of one file and deposit them in another. It takes the form:

```
SORT FROM THISFILE TO THATFILE
```

Try this example with the Workbench disk as the current directory:

```
LIST TO RAM:UNSORTED ALL

SORT RAM:UNSORTED RAM:SORTED

ED RAM:SORTED
```

Hey presto an alphabetical list of contents of the entire Workbench disk. If you didn't quite catch all that was going on, here's a brief explanation. Using the "ALL" option with LIST enables a complete compendium of the disk's contents to be produced including the contents of each directory. This is directed to the file "UNSORTED" on the Ram Disk. An added bonus is that as there is no such file already in existence, it creates a file of that name. Beware if there is already such a file as it will be over-written!

The SORT command then sifts through the contents of the UNSORTED file, arranges the lines in alphabetical order and deposits this new ordering in another new file "SORTED". Finally, loading this into ED lets us view the results.

You can also use the command to SORT a file to itself by the:

```
SORT THIS THIS
```

approach. The danger of this is that it overwrites the original "THIS" file which may not have been what you desired...

Join the Club

A very straightforward means of appending one (or more) file to another is to use the JOIN command. To glue files: "FILE1", "FILE2" and "FILE3" together requires just the:

```
JOIN FILE1 FILE2 FILE3 TO FILE4
```

command. The file "FILE4" is created. However, if a "FILE4" already exists then it will be overwritten, so check before JOINing.

Flexible Programs

It's all very well writing scripts that can cope with situations that we can predict but quite often things aren't quite so rigid. In these cases a program is needed that can deal with different eventualities. If situation A arises then it takes one course of action, if situation B arises then it takes another. Even more sophisticated are programs that stop and ask the user for some input: "What should I do next – A, B or C?" Surprise, surprise – AmigaDOS is equipped with commands that allow just that to be done.

IF...ELSE...

The mechanism of IF and ELSE commands is central to script writing and its implementation is simple.

```
IF [condition A exists]
    [DO THIS ACTION]
ELSE
    [DO THE OTHER ACTION]
ENDIF
```

What "condition A" is and what "THIS" and "THE OTHER" actions are is up to the programmer. The Startup-Sequence, for example, checks to see if there is a "User Startup" file. IF there is then it is EXECUTEd, ELSE this line is ignored:

```
IF EXISTS S:User-Startup
    Execute S:User-Startup
ENDIF
```

As you can see this example does not use the ELSE command as AmigaDOS is designed to do nothing in its absence (the null option). The whole process of stating IF... DO THIS, ELSE DO THE OTHER often goes under the title of "condition testing".

Choice Request

This has to be the easiest way to produce an interactive script file known to mankind.

Using REQUESTCHOICE you can make the script file ask a question and depending on the answer, perform different tasks. REQUESTCHOICE pops up a request box onto the Workbench screen with a selection of buttons to press. This is done by a relatively straightforward but lengthy command on the lines of:

```
REQUESTCHOICE >ENV:VARIABLE "TITLE" "QUESTION"
"OPTION1" "OPTION2" "OPTION3" "CANCEL"
```

When used in a script this little snippet will put up a request box with the heading "TITLE", asking the question "QUESTION" and with four buttons to choose from labelled as "OPTION1" "OPTION2" "OPTION3" and "CANCEL". Depending on which of the options is clicked on, the variable called "VARIABLE" is assigned a value of 1, 2, 3 or 0 in that order. Hence "CANCEL" being placed as the last option. The program can then deal with these responses in a series of IF and ENDIF clauses as follows:

```
REQUESTCHOICE >ENV:VARIABLE "TITLE" "QUESTION"
"OPTION1" "OPTION2" "OPTION3" "CANCEL"

IF $VARIABLE EQ 0    ;"CANCEL"
DO ACTION A     ;whatever that is
ENDIF
IF $VARIABLE EQ 1    ;"OPTION1"
DO ACTION B     ;whatever that is
ENDIF
IF $VARIABLE EQ 2    ;"OPTION2"
DO ACTION C     ;whatever that is
ENDIF
IF $VARIABLE EQ 3    ;"OPTION3"
DO ACTION D     ;whatever that is
ENDIF
```

Insider Guide #13: Using REQUESTCHOICE.

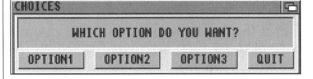

REQUESTCHOICE enables a script to ask the user for various input options. Each option is related to a different value of variable "THIS".

*Option
0 is the
"Quit"
or
"Cancel"
option.*

```
REQUESTCHOICE >ENV:THIS "CHOICES" "WHICH OPTION DO YOU WANT?" "OPTION1" "OPTI
IF $THIS EQ "0"
ECHO "GOODBYE"
ENDIF
IF $THIS EQ "1"
ECHO "YOU CHOSE OPTION 1"
ENDIF
IF $THIS EQ "2"
ECHO "YOU CHOSE OPTION 2"
ENDIF
IF $THIS EQ "3"
ECHO " YOU CHOSE OPTION3"
ENDIF
```

CHOICES

WHICH OPTION DO YOU WANT?

| OPTION1 | OPTION2 | OPTION3 | QUIT |

*Any others
allow some
function to
be carried
out.*

REQUESTCHOICE produces a box appropriately titled, asking a question and with the choices presented as a series of "buttons".

AmigaDOS translates a button-click into an operation included within the script. In this case the user is then returned to the Shell window.

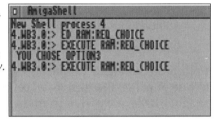

```
AmigaShell
New Shell process 4
4.WB3.0:> ED RAM:REQ_CHOICE
4.WB3.0:> EXECUTE RAM:REQ_CHOICE
 YOU CHOSE OPTION3
4.WB3.0:> EXECUTE RAM:REQ_CHOICE
```

INSTALL

When the Workbench disk is inserted into the disk drive on startup the A1200 accepts it and starts looking for files to tell it how it should go about the startup process. Put in any other disk and it is ignored. The difference is that Workbench has been designated as a "boot" disk by using the INSTALL command. Any device can be so assigned, simply by using the:

```
INSTALL DF0:
```

command. Thus, if you wish to make another boot disk by copying some of the Workbench files to another disk, that disk will need to be INSTALLed before it can be used to boot from.

ADDBUFFERS

A buffer is a small amount of memory (RAM) that can be used to store information in. In this case the information stored is details about a disk's contents. When you double-click on a disk icon it reads the root directory of that disk and displays it on the Workbench screen. As reading from disks is physically slow, this information can be stored in RAM so that, should the information be required again – as it inevitably will – the whole process does not need repeating. Instead it is taken from the RAM buffer. By default all floppy disk drives have a setting of "5 buffers" but this is increased for DF0: in the Startup-Sequence by a further 15. The buffer settings can be read by typing in:

```
ADDBUFFERS DF0:

DF0: has 20 buffers
```

and altered by something along the lines of:

```
ADDBUFFERS DF1: 10

DF1: has 15 buffers
```

or

```
ADDBUFFERS DF0: -5

DF0: has 15 buffers
```

In practice a setting of 25 should be enough for any drive. With each increase of buffer size there is, of course, a proportionate decrease in available RAM. Bear this in mind before rewriting the Startup-Sequence file.

MOUNT

The most common use of this command will be with the RAD disk as in:

```
MOUNT RAD:
```

However unless you are using a hard disk you will first have to type in:

```
PATH STORAGE:DOSDRIVERS
```

Insider Guide #14: ReadMe files with More – Part 1

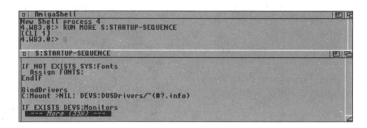

The first step is to choose – or write – the file that you want displayed. Where better to start than the startup-sequence file on the Workbench disk? As it is unwise to attempt to play around with anything so essential to the A1200 we will use a copy of this file.

1> COPY SYS:S/STARTUP-SEQUENCE TO RAM:TEXT

The next thing we need is a script file which will read the "TEXT" file. Use the ED utility to create a ReadMe file

ED RAM:README

As the MORE command is so direct in its approach this "program" need be of just one line

RUN MORE TEXT

Save this by pressing <ESC> then <X>.

What we now have on the Ram Disk are two files "Text" and "ReadMe". The ReadMe script can be used to display the Text file. To do this demands that the A1200 knows that the ReadMe file is a script file. This can be done using the PROTECT command:

PROTECT RAM:README +S

PROTECT RAM:README +E

The second of these makes the file "executable". This will now work from the Workbench provided that the "Show>>All Files" option has been highlighted. Try it and see. What happens is an "Execute a File" window pops up asking for any command arguments to be added to the ReadMe command. But, so far, this is hardly any more convenient than using the "Execute a Command" option to enter the RUN MORE TEXT command.

This gets the RAD disk up and running and it can be as easily removed with the one word command:

REMRAD

Insider Guide #15: ReadMe files with More – Part 2

```
□  s
; $VER: startup-sequence 39.9 (9.8.92)

C:SetPatch QUIET
C:Version >NIL:
C:AddBuffers >NIL: DF0: 15
FailAt 21

C:MakeDir RAM:T RAM:Clipboards RAM:ENV RAM:EN
C:Copy >NIL: ENVARC: RAM:ENV ALL NOREQ

Resident >NIL: C:Assign PURE
Resident >NIL: C:Execute PURE
--- More (21%) ---
```

To make the whole thing more professional, the program needs a ReadMe icon which is visible at all times and for this to launch the text file viewer when double-clicked.

Files are only ever visible on the Workbench when there is a .info file associated with them. As the "Show>>Only Icons" option is chosen on the Workbench by default any files that are normally visible will be those that have .info files associated with them. As these icons can represent disks, directories, projects, tools and the trashcan they have different properties. These can be studied by clicking on the icon in question and then selecting the "Information" option from the Workbench "Icons" menu.

To run a script what is needed is something which will recognise that that is what is trying to be achieved. When the icon is double-clicked we want the A1200 to understand that it has to find a script file of that name, open a window and plonk the output into it. ICONX is the man for the job. This AmigaDOS command does just what we want. All we need now is a .info file that can have ICONX set as its default tool. The standard route to this end is to create a copy of the .info file associated with the Shell utility.

COPY SYS:SYSTEM/SHELL.INFO RAM:README.INFO

This creates a copy of the Shell icon on the Ram Disk but with the name "ReadMe". Should you double-click on this it will still launch the Shell window. This is because the Default Tool in the Information window is "SYS:SYSTEM/CLI"

Thus when the ReadMe icon is double-clicked it goes away and opens a Shell window. Changing the default tool to C:ICONX means that it goes away and looks for a script file of the same name to launch in a window. Hooray!

Now when the ReadMe icon is double-clicked it produces a MORE listing of the Startup-Sequence file.

Using AmigaDOS without leaving the Workbench is sacrilege to some but it's salvation for the Shell-shocked...

```
□ | RAM:WBLIST
Directory "DF0:" on Wednesday 02-Sep-92
Classes                          Dir ----rwed To
Expansion                        Dir ----rwed To
System                           Dir ----rwed To
Rexxc                            Dir ----rwed To
Utilities                        Dir ----rwed To
L                                Dir ----rwed To
S                                Dir ----rwed To
Devs.info                        632 ----rw-d To
Expansion.info                   632 ----rw-d To
Prefs.info                       724 ----rw-d To
System.info                      632 ----rw-d To
Utilities.info                   632 ----rw-d To
WBStartup.info                   632 ----rw-d To
Disk.info                        388 ----rw-d To
```

*T*he increased use of AmigaDOS goes hand in hand with increased use of the Amiga. If this area of A1200 use is up your street then the chapters already reached on AmigaDOS should be to your liking. However, this isn't the case for everyone...

Cracking the Shell

If typing in obscure computer commands leaves you cold there will still be many occasions when the quickest way to achieve results is via AmigaDOS. Fear not, however, because in this chapter I have assembled some of the more commonly used AmigaDOS "One-Liners". You can use them without leaving the safety of the Workbench. If you're cautious in your enthusiasm for AmigaDOS then this provides a relatively painless way into the subject.

The Workbench menu has an "Execute Command..." option which can also be invoked by the <Amiga><E> hot-key combination. It allows commands of over 100 characters to be entered which should be far more than you'll ever need. If you use commands of more than 33 characters the start of the command line starts scrolling out of the file requester as you type in at the righthand end.

File Display

Files can be viewed in a number of ways. MultiView, in particular, is a very useful way of showing the contents of a file – assuming it recognises the file type. TYPE is another and much more rough and ready way of viewing a file. It simply deposits the contents of a file into a viewer. As such TYPE makes no effort to understand the file, it simply shows what is there. If the file is gibberish then TYPE will display gibberish. This doesn't immediately recommend itself for use but in fact can be handy when you're searching through a batch of files and have no idea what sort of files they are. MultiView by comparison chickens out of its responsibilities by displaying its "Unknown data type for..." messages. Not much use if you're trying to determine whether the file you have in front of you comes from a wordprocessor or a graphics package.

The TYPE syntax is simply:

    TYPE DF0:FILENAME

A more sophisticated approach is offered by the similar:

    MORE DF0:FILENAME

Like TYPE, MORE can display all sorts of meaningless binary code – if that's what you want. Files can also be joined together (*concatenated* in the jargon) by using the command:

    JOIN FILE1 FILE2 FILE3 AS FILE4

Making Dates

No, this isn't an introduction to computer dating but you can use your A1200 to get the date. For example, typing in the following AmigaDOS command at the Shell prompt:

    DATE

gets the A1200 to report back what it thinks the date and time is. Typing in:

```
DATE DD-MMM-YY HH:MM:SS
```

as in:

```
DATE 25-DEC-94 15:30:12
```

updates it to whatever the current date really is. Why bother? Well, when you save a file it is saved with a record of the date when it was last saved. This information can be very handy if you're, say, searching for a letter you wrote to the bank manager in April as opposed to all the other ones you wrote every other month.

On the List

LIST is one of AmigaDOS's most powerful and often-used commands. Strange then to find it in a chapter which is aimed at DOSophobes. The excuse is that although the information it supplies can be obtained through conventional Workbench methods it is often easier to use a LIST command.

For example:

```
LIST RAM: ALL
```

supplies details of not just the Ram Disk's root directory (the one you see when you double-click on the Ram Disk icon) but also of the contents of each and every subdirectory and includes any FILENOTES that have been added. It would take ages to do that on the Workbench and even when you did you would require endless use of the Information window to be as well informed.

The only danger with the LIST command as it stands is the risk of being overwhelmed by the information it supplies. Try:

```
LIST SYS:ALL
```

and you will see what I mean. The way out is to direct the output of the command to a file such as:

```
LIST RAM: ALL >RAM:FILE
```

or

```
LIST RAM: ALL TO RAM:FILE
```

Which puts all the details into the "FILE" where it can be read at leisure – for example by using:

MORE RAM:FILE

Make sure that there is a space between the first "RAM:" and "ALL" in the last example. You might like to see what happens if you don't: firstly when there isn't, and secondly when there is, a file on the Ram Disk called "ALL".

Making Notes

Computing is a means of creating more and more files. Some useful but others less so. There is a danger of being swamped by the less-used files and, if they're not binned, it does no harm to put them into cold storage. Trouble is that when you start looking for that file you made months ago it's very difficult to remember, for example, what "ANGLETBANOD" had in it. FILENOTE comes into its own here because if you had used the Execute Command to append this as a file note:

FILENOTE FILE "ANGRY LETTER TO BANK RE: OVER-DRAFT"

you would be able to view the results through the Information window or through a LIST command...

Forced Eviction

There are many occasions when you wish to delete an entire directory and its contents. If you are sure this is what you wish to do then click on it and select "Delete" from the icons menu. However, this will fail if one or more files in the directory are protected against deletion. One solution would be to go through, find out which ones are protected and then change this characteristic in the "Information" window associated with each file. But if you don't want to be at it until next Christmas try:

DELETE DIRECTORY ALL FORCE

which ignores any file protectors and deletes anyway. Be careful with this one, though, as there's often a good reason why a file has been protected in the first place.

Insider Guide #16: Using LIST to create files.

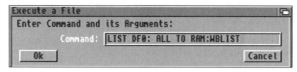

You can use the LIST command to create files.

1. *Place the Workbench disk in the internal drive.*

2. *Use the Execute Command... option and type in:*

LIST DF0: ALL TO RAM:WBLIST

3. Once this has finished, double-click on the Ram Disk icon. Select "Show >> All Files" from the Workbench Window menu.

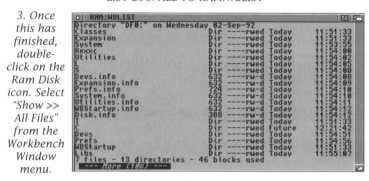

4. *To view the file use the Execute Command... interface once more and type in:*

MORE RAM:WBLIST

The end result is a directory listing of every single directory and file on the Workbench disk.

5. *By this point you should be wondering if there isn't a faster way of doing all this. There is – but it's called the Shell.*

More Protections

The A1200 lets you LOCK a device, ie hard drive or internal drive, against deleting anything on it. The syntax for this is very straightforward:

LOCK DF0: ON

but its use is less obvious. It could be one way of letting a child get its sticky hands onto your computer without worrying about it trashing all your files.

INFO

As its name suggests INFO provides information to the user. The information provided is about the filing system being used and the disk devices that are currently being used. This is all done with the simple one word command:

INFO

One step up from this would be to direct the output to a file should you want to keep a record of what is going on:

INFO >RAM:INFOFILE

MAKEDIR

On the Workbench there is a perfectly good directory creator "New Drawer" which is found in the "Windows" directory and which can be accessed via the <Amiga><N> hotkey combination. As we have seen this actually creates two files: one being the directory the other being the .info file associated with it. The drawers (the visible directories) should be used for storing anything that you need to use on a regular basis. Invisible drawers (directories) should be used for storing data that you don't use but the A1200 often does. The easiest way to create such a directory is via the:

MAKEDIR RAM:NEW

sort of command.

Speed Reading

When a disk is read, the information about the files it holds are stored in a cache. This is a small segment of memory put aside for this purpose and is, by default, approximately 11K in size.

To demonstrate this in practice, soft-reboot the A1200 by pressing <CTRL><Amiga><Amiga> and then double-click on the Workbench disk icon. There is a short pause while the disk is read and its contents displayed to screen in a window. Close that window and repeat the process. What you should notice is that the process is slightly quicker second time round. The reason being that the A1200 has inspected the sector cache first to see if the information it is seeking can be found there rather than reading the floppy disk which it knows to be a slow and painful operation. Try:

ADDBUFFERS DFO: 25

and repeat the process for an exaggerated display of how ADDBUFFERS works – all the information is now held in cache which can be read faster than the floppy disk.

STATUS

Absolutely nothing to do with prestige, STATUS lets you know what you're A1200 is up to. As I was writing this it reported back to me:

Process 1: Loaded as command: status

Process 2: Loaded as command: C:ConClip

Process 3: Loaded as command: Workbench

Which lets me keep an eye on what it's up to. Being a multi-tasking machine it is capable of running several processes at once – or giving the appearance of so doing. Here I am doing next to nothing with it and it reports back three activities.

Copy Cats

The Workbench system of copying disks is slow and inflexible and is better done using AmigaDOS. The following is the AmigaDOS duffer's guide to disk copying from the "Execute Command..." interface.

With one disk drive:

You need the RAD disk mounted and then just type in:

DISKCOPY DFO: RAD:

which copies the disk in the internal drive to the RAD disk. Put the second disk into the internal drive and then type in:

DISKCOPY RAD: DFO:

and the process is complete, thus saving about six or seven disk swaps.

If you don't have the RAD disk mounted try:

COPY DFO: RAM: ALL CLONE

COPY RAM: DFO: ALL CLONE

This will copy all the files across but won't change the name of the disk itself and nor will it make the copy into a boot disk. To do this requires yet another command:

INSTALL DF0:

However, this is still quicker than using Workbench.

With two disk drives use:

DISKCOPY DF0: DF1:

life doesn't come much easier.

Launching Apps

If an application is on one of the A1200's paths then it can be launched just by typing in its name at the "Execute Command..." interface. If you are using an internal drive only set-up then this restricts you to whatever is on the boot disk. If that is the Workbench disk then that means just MultiView, Clock, EDIT and ED. However, even with these an advantage can be gained over the Workbench system because MultiView can be made to display to a separate screen using the:

MULTIVIEW FILENAME SCREEN

command. Thus if it is a picture employing more colours than available on the Workbench it will retain those extra colours.

If you are blessed with a hard drive then all Preference editors, Tools, Commodities and System programs can be launched from the "Execute Command..." interface. This can't be done with a two drive system. Any alterations to PATH only exist as long as that Shell window (or Execute Command... window) is open.

**Printing is easy but printing *well* can require
lengthy experimentation with all manner of
options unless you know what you're doing...**

```
Printer Preferences
         Printer Type              Printer Port:  [↻]    Parallel
 EpsonX                            Print Pitch:   [↻]  Elite (12 cpi
 Generic
 PostScript                        Print Spacing: [↻] 8 Lines Per In
                                   Print Quality: [↻]    Letter
                                    Paper Type:   [↻]    Single
                                   Paper Format:  [↻]    DIN A4

                                 Paper Length (lines)    : [6
                                 Left Margin (characters): [5
                                 Right Margin (characters): [4
```

*A*lmost every computer user wants to use a printer at
some stage or other but few relish the prospect. Why?
Because getting your computer/printer combination to
print out exactly what you want it to invariably involves playing around with sheets of paper, adjusting set-ups here and
there and a fair degree of cursing.

The main problem is one of choice. Now it's all very well to
have a wide choice but when you don't know the hows and
whys of those choices, making a decision is very difficult. In
the realm of printers there are choices galore.

For starters there are several different types of printer: dot-
matrix, inkjet, laser and daisy wheel, all made by a great number of different manufacturers. Some are of these are colour,
some black-and-white, some can print on wide paper, some
come provided with mechanisms for controlling the thoughput
of paper, some have lengthy lists of options and detailed manu-
als and some have none of these.

Bearing all this in mind, what follows can only be a rough guide to getting your printer going. There are no substitutes to sitting down and experimenting with all the settings to get decent results on your own printer. If at the end of this chapter you still don't know what's going on and you can't get anything to print then help is at hand in the form of Robin Burton's *Mastering Amiga Printers* which just so happens to be available from Bruce Smith Books.

For the following examples I used a Star LC-200. It's a colour dot-matrix printer of the type that most A1200 owners will use.

Unpacking

Once you are the proud owner of a shiny new printer the first step is to take it out of its wrappings and attach it to a power source. It should come equipped with a cable to connect it with the A1200's parallel port and a couple of printer ribbon cartridges.

The Star LC-200 is a colour printer but here I'm only interested in mono printing so I'll use the black ribbon which fits neatly into place. What else is there? Usually some sort of paper feeder which somehow clips into place.

Most cheap printers can be fed paper in the same way as you would a typewriter so that the top of the paper is underneath the business part of the printhead. The LC-200 – and most printers like it – will even do this part for you. The printer's control panel should include various buttons including one entitled "On Line" and one called "Paper Feed"; these should have little lights associated with them.

When the "On Line" light is on, the printer is all hooked up and waiting for something to print. Press the "On Line" button and this light goes out. Now, pressing the "Paper Feed" button automatically positions a sheet of paper in the correct place. Press the "On Line" button again and we're ready to go.

Most printers will be able to cope with specialised computer paper. This comes on a continuous strip of sheets each with tear-off strips down the side punched with holes. If you are using this sort of set-up then the printer will take all the worry about positioning the paper. The printer will have plastic "teeth" to attach the paper to. This is usually called "tractor feeding".

Not all printers will have this sort of set-up although most should have something remarkably similar even if only as an optional extra – ie more expense. If you are using ordinary sheets of paper there shold be some clip-on guides for feeding paper into the right place. Although the printer should position each sheet correctly in terms of vertical alignment, it is often up to you to set it correctly for left or right positioning. Make a note of where you have positioned it and, if you find later on that part of your print out has disappeared off the edge of the paper, you can make sure that any subsequent sheets are positioned more accurately. If it has been said once it's been said a thousand times: experiment!

Choosing a Driver

The next step is to set up the A1200 so that it can translate any file that we might want to print into a form that the printer can understand.

The piece of software that performs this magic is called a *printer driver* and can be found in the Printers directory on the Storage disk. As you will see, there is quite a number to choose from all bearing the name of one type of printer or another. If there is one with the name of your printer then copy this into the Devs/Printers directory on your Workbench disk. Sadly none say "Star" or "LC-200" never mind both so what is there to do?

The A1200 comes supplied with a printer driver called "Generic" which has been designed to work with most major types of printer. If this doesn't work then try using a printer driver for a printer similar to your own: many dot-matrix printers are *Epson-compatible* so called because they work in a near identical manner to an Epson printer. Similarly, ink jet printers often work to a *Hewlett-Packard* standard.

The printer drivers in the Storage disk are not an exhaustive list of those suitable for use on the A1200. Others may be available from PD libraries or commercial sources. Printers are often supplied with the appropriate printer driver – contact the manufacturers if you draw a blank elsewhere.

If you haven't yet bought a printer then before you part with your money, check that there is a suitable driver for it that works on an Amiga A1200. If there isn't – or if the dealer isn't sure but thinks it will "probably work" with a different one – then consider buying a different printer.

Having done all that, we now need the Preferences directory on the Extras disk. In there is a utility called Printer. Double-click on its icon and a window should pop-up with a range of choices. Most important amongst these for the time being is the list of Printer Types in the left-hand column.

Printer Bugs

Ignore this section if, when you launched the Printer utility, the Printer Types column contained a list of the printer drivers available to you – just like it is supposed to. However, if this window is empty then you have stumbled across a software *bug*. The "Printer" Preferences utility that was originally shipped with the A1200 was not a perfectly written piece of software. If you are using it with a standard A1200 without any additional hard drive or floppy drive then, when it is launched it does not correctly read the contents of the Workbench disk Devs/Printers directory. The best way round this is to copy the "Printers" tool from the Extras disk onto the Ram Disk. Replace the Workbench disk in the internal drive and now, when you launch the utility, the printer drivers are there and waiting.

At some stage Commodore might get round to producing an update and improved version of this preferences tool. If it does then you won't have any of the problems outlined above.

Printing Text Files

With a list of printer drivers finally available, click on the one you want to use, make sure the "Printer Port" (top right) is set to "Parallel" and then click on the "Save" button. With this all done it's about time to print a document. I've used the Startup-Sequence file but any text-only file will do. Load this into MultiView and choose Print from MultiView's Project menu. At this point the printer should leap into action and race away printing out the file. A system request window will also pop-up on screen offerring the opportunity to "Abort" the operation. Just sit back and watch as your printer churns out a page of text.

This should print out a page of plain text. However, you also have control over where the text is placed on the page, the size and quality of text and and the number of lines of text per inch. Go back to the Printer Preferences editor and adjust the settings of the "Print Pitch",

"Print Spacing", Print Quality" and "Paper Length" and margins to suit your choice. Click on "Use", then double-click on the "InitPrinter" device in the Tools directory and then print.

Printing Graphics

A graphics file is one which contains pictures. The procedure is pretty much the same as for printing a text file except that this time the PrinterGFX tool is used. Although straightforward enough to use the list of options is bewildering: Dithering (Ordered, Halftone or Floyd-Steinberg); Scaling (Fraction or Integer); Image (Positive or Negative); Aspect (Horizontal or Vertical); Shade (Black & White, Grey Scale 1, Grey Scale 2 or Color); Threshold (1 to 15); Density (1 to 7); Smoothing (On or Off); and Center Picture (On or Off). That's a lot of possible combinations.

As they can all have a profound effect on the final image some lengthy experimentation is called for. If you are going to set out down this route – which you should if you want to achieve decent results – then let me suggest you use a small picture to play around with. The effects of most of the variables are illustrated in the Figure 12.2 overleaf.

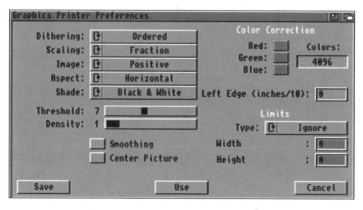

Figure 12.1. PrinterGFX Preference editor.

Trouble-shooting

Supposing nothing happened. If you've followed the steps above and not printed anything out then don't fret. The solution is probably very straightforward. The first things to check are all the obvious ones. Is everything plugged in and switched on properly? Is the cable connecting printer to computer fitting snug-

Adjusting the settings in the PrinterGfx Preference utility is the best way of achieving better print-outs.

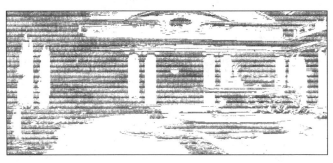

1. Print out using the default settings and view the result. Don't worry about the aspect ratio at this stage.

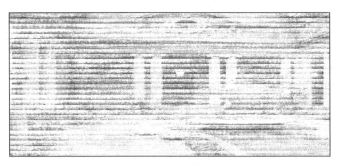

2. Choosing one of the grey scale options increases the number of grey tints in the image.

3. Adjusting the dithering option produces subtle changes – Floyd-Steinberg has been used here.

Figure 12.2. Using PrinterGFX's Preference settings.

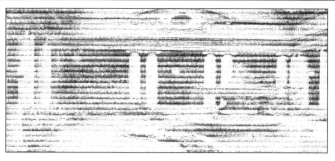

4. The image is still weak. Altering the density and threshold values should beef it up a little; this uses a Density of 2 and a Threshold setting of 10.

5. Alter the Limits values to correct the image size and shape. I've used the Multiply values of 2 (width) and 4 (height).

gly at both ends? Is the "On Line" light on the printer switched on? If not, it should be. Did the printer bleep at you when you tried to print? If so then the paper is probably not correctly fitted – try playing around with it. You may still encounter problems printing a file:

a)   It printed out but it's gibberish and bears no relation to the original file. Try a different printer driver.

b) It printed out but some of the text is missing off the edge of the paper. Reposition the paper next time you print. Trial and error yet again.

c) The Preference settings haven't worked. This is a common problem if you are trying to use the "Generic" printer driver. Although the Printer Preferences allow you to make all sorts of decisions about the size of letters, the quality of print and the position of margins, these are all ignored in practice. This is because "Generic" is rough and ready in its approach and only serves to produce some (any) output. If you want anything more than this then you'll have to find an appropriate printer driver.

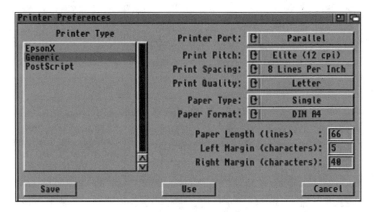

Figure 12.3. Printer Preference editor.

d) Words are broken at the end of lines. Set the page width (Left margin - Right margin) so that it is the same as the number of characters per line in the original document.

e) Margins. With the lefthand margin set to zero, printing should start right on the lefthand edge of the paper. If it doesn't, then adjust the lateral movement of the paper feeder until it does. Similarly printing should be possible right from the very top of the paper though this is normally controlled by the printer itself.

Driver Workings

Just how does a printer driver work? I have a document I want to print. There is a printer attached to my A1200. I need a piece of software that can look at that document, understand what it represents and then send a series of messages to the printer so that the printer makes appropriate marks on a piece of paper. The printer is not involved in any of this interpretation business. It just sits there awaiting instructions. If those instructions tell it to print gibberish then it will print gibberish. Should all the information arrive as you planned it then the printer output will look remarkably like you intended.

So to print out a MultiView document a process something like the following happens. The A1200 checks from the Printer Preferences file what sort of printer is attached. It then prepares the output in a manner that that printer can understand. It next checks that the printer is connected, switched on and loaded with paper and sends it the first set of instructions about what to print. Once these have been executed the printer then says that it's ready for the next bit which the A1200 dutifully churns out. This process continues until the end of the document is reached. Sometimes the process has to be halted while the user loads another sheet or two of paper but the A1200 is aware that this is what is happening and holds onto its data accordingly.

At no stage during this whole process does the printer need to be concerned with what machine is attached to the other end of its printer cable. As long as the messages being passed to it down the wire make sense then it will print out whatever it is told to do. It is as if the printer speaks its own language and it is the job of the computer to do all the translating work.

Now this whole process can be a bit slow. The A1200 can prepare the information to print fast enough but if it keeps having to wait while the printer does one line of work before asking for another then we're going to be here all day. Many of the larger printers have a store of their own internal memory so that, except for really mammoth files, the whole lot can be sent down to the printer in one fell swoop leaving the computer to get on with the next task in hand. If you have a printer like that then bully for you. However, the rest of us still have one or two aces up our sleeves.

If the slow part of printing is the printer and not the computer then there's no reason why we cannot plan for this. The printout process can be split up into two parts: Part One is the preparation of data into a form that the printer can understand; Part Two is the sending of that data to the printer. Parts One or Two can be done weeks apart if need be. Not only that but they need not even be done on the same machine!

What this means in practice is that you can use your A1200 to prepare a file for printing to one particular type of printer and save that file on a disk. Then when you're not wanting to use your printer for something else you can set it up to print out all these files you have been accumulating. Better still you don't even need to have a printer yourself. You just pop round to your friends' house with the disk and use their machine. And this is the clever bit. As the printer file is of a type that only has to be understood by the printer it isn't important which sort of computer your friends have – as long as it can read the disk and you've used the correct printer driver then any old machine will do. This process is called printing to a file.

Change Device

Printing, particularly of large graphics files can be a slow business. One way round this is to print everything you want to files and then, at the end of a session send these files to a printer. The advantage of this approach is that these files can even be transferred from one machine to another as long as they have been designed for the appropriate printer driver.

To print to a file requires the CMD (Change Main Device) utility which is found in the Tools directory.

Click on it once and then open it's Information window from the Workbench Icons menu. There are five tool types associated with this utility, each with a different setting which can be adjusted. Change SKIP=FALSE to SKIP=TRUE, and "Save" that change. Now double-click on the CMD icon and when the next file is printed it is redirected to a file on the Ram Disk called "CMD_file". This destination can also be altered to suit your own needs.

To print such a file use the command:

```
PRINTFILES RAM:CMD_FILE
```

Multiple files can be printed using this command in the format:

```
PRINTFILES -F FILE1 FILE2 FILE3 FILE4
```

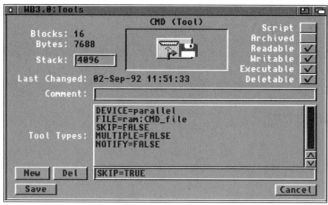

Insider Guide #17: Using someone else's printer.

Choose the printer you are going to print out on and select the relevant Amiga printer driver. If this is not on the Storage disk then you will need to obtain it from a commercial source.

1. Load the printer driver into the Devs/Printers directory on your Workbench disk.

2. From Preferences select that driver as the default option.

3. Load the CMD device and change its Default Tool setting to SKIP=TRUE

4. Print your file.

5. The result is stored on the Ram Disk as "CMD_file". Copy this to disk and transfer to whichever computer is connected to the high quality printer. For example, that PC at work...

where the -F suffix executes a *form feed* which ensures that each new file starts printing from the top of a new sheet of paper – this presupposes that the *first* sheet was correctly placed.

Experiment!

There's no substitute for experimentation. The images in this chapter have been created on the Star LC-200 printer. The results on your machine may be considerably different. I know it sounds obvious but you will save a lot of printer wear and tear, paper and time if you use a *small* picture!

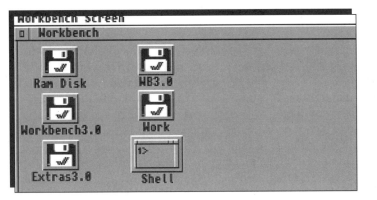

Turn your ugly duckling A1200 into a beautiful swan and learn how to fly...

*T*he A1200 as supplied comprises the machine itself, a power supply, some Workbench disks, a mouse, a rather inadequate user's manual and an assortment of cables and leads. Throw in some software and it's enough to keep you happy for several months or even years. For most users though the supppled pack is insufficient for their needs and various extras are craved.

Like most hobbies Computing has this habit of requiring more and more money. You spend several hundred pounds buying the computer intending to use it for one particular aspect and then discover that there are no end of other potential uses for the machine. The trouble is that to get the most out of these potentials requires buying bits and pieces.

The first addition most people make to their machines is an extra helping of memory (RAM) and an additional drive: be it floppy drive or hard drive. As these are so commonplace three chapters have been devoted to these issues: "Improve Your Memory", "Not So Hard After All" and "A Hard Act To Follow".

That's not all: the hardware add-ons for writing and playing music are discussed in the "Sounds Good" chapter, monitors are covered in the "Put It On Display" chapter and genlocks and digitisers in "Moving Pictures". The following then covers the other choices available to you. If you're looking to economise then don't read on...

But if you're not shy of stretching the old purse-strings that bit further or you want to dream of what to spend the cash on when your boat comes in then the following is intended as a brief overview of what's available.

Extra Disk Drive

If you're still struggling with the base machine then you will frequently be irritated by the number of times that a prompt requests you to insert a disk into the drive. No sooner have you done that than the machine whirrs and grinds for a few seconds before demanding a different disk. Put that disk in and it's a few more minutes of grinding before the first disk is demanded again – can't the machine make up its mind? All of which makes the whole process irritatingly slow. Buying an extra floppy disk drive is just one of the ways round this problem. When the machine wants a particular disk you just slot it into the spare drive. OK there will always be occasions when the machine wants to access a third disk but the time saved is genuine enough in most circumstances.

Almost all extra disk drives duplicate the ability of the internal drive but you can now buy high density disk drives. These take 3.5 inch disks that look remarkably like any other but which can be formatted to take 1.4Mb of data. The visible difference is a small hole on the opposite side of the disk to the write-protect tab. High Density (HD) disks can be formatted in the internal drive to 880K but that is a bit of a waste. Similarly the lower density disks can be read by a high density drive. What you can't do is read a 1.4Mb disk in the standard internal drive – it just isn't mechanically up to the job.

An extra disk drive is a cheap enough purchase – typically £50 or so – and could be just what you are looking for. A word of caution, though. Before rushing out and buying that extra drive consider the other options available to you. Some hard drive units aren't that much more so think carefully over whether it wouldn't be worth saving up for the latter with all the additional benefits that it offers.

Rapid Expansion

This may seem like a daft question, but are you finding your A1200 too slow? If you are new to the Amiga or have upgraded from an earlier model then the very thought of the A1200 with its 32-bit custom graphics chips being thought slow may horrify you and before going any further we have to establish what we mean. Certain aspects of computing are slow – reading a floppy disk for example – and there are numerous ways of speeding up computing as a whole without making any difference to how fast the processors are working.

More memory, an extra floppy drive, different software, a hard disk, using the RAD disk and the Fast Filing System – there are many ways to improve matters and all are covered elsewhere in this book. But what we're concerned with here is making the machine itself physically go faster.

All technologies have their limits and there are certain uses of the A1200 which require the machine to make vast numbers of calculations. Ray-tracing is one such example. If you haven't come across this before then ray-tracing is a means of creating those brighter than life illustrations where a chromium ball is balanced above a multi-coloured tiled floor or something equally plausible. The reason they look so technically perfect is because they are. The path of each ray of light has been calculated to establish where each shadow falls, what reflections will be made and how brightly lit each component is as a result. That's a lot of mathematics and regular users of raytracing programs are used to inordinate waits while their machines painfully run through thousands, millions, of mind-numbing calculations before drawing the latest version of the picture. Multiply that time when you're trying to create an animation from a sequence of such pictures and you'll start wondering if there isn't something better you could be doing with your time rather than waiting for machines to do big sums.

Flight simulations are another typical beneficiary of faster processing as are fractal generators and desktop publishers. In fact any application which uses a lot of memory and requires large numbers of calculations to be made can benefit from a faster processor so, if you are regularly using and manipulating particularly large databases or spreadsheets then this could be for you.

Choice of accelerators on the A1200 is more restricted than for some other computers for the very good reason that it is already equipped with a fast processor – the 14MHz 68020. Fitting an accelerator card built around the 68030 processor running at a typical 40MHz should speed things about fourfold. An accelerator card and extra RAM card usually fits via the A1200 trap-door.

FPUs and Co-pros

A faster processor isn't the only option – there is also a maths co-processor to consider. As its name suggests, this runs in parallel with the A1200's processor chip and takes on the task of doing all those calculations that include fractions. (As this entails using decimal points, the maths co-processor is also refered to as a Floating Point Unit or FPU.) A maths co-processor is usually available as an addition to an accelerator card and may be worth considering when purchasing if you really need speed. Choose the 68882 (rather than its 68881 predecessor) as it was designed with the 68030 in mind and is consequently much faster.

Other options include extra RAM and even a hard disk as accelerator cards can be bought as part of a larger upgrade to bolt-on to the A1200.

Joysticks

If you're into games playing then you'll want a joystick and you can pick a decent one up for as little as a tenner. If you're a total couch potato you can even spend several hundred pounds on a state-of-the-art armchair with joystick built in to one of its armrests – you pays your money and takes your choice. The more games orientated Amiga magazines – Amiga Power, Amiga Force et al – have periodic reviews of which joystick is best at the price.

Printers

Obviously if you are using a word-processor or Desktop Publisher you'll want a printed version of any work you produce. After all, there's not much point writing a letter on your machine if you can't send it to anyone! The subject of printers is a bit of a minefield. There are so many different models to choose from all with different capabilities that it can be a hard task trying to decide what is best for you. Again the magazine reviews should be helpful.

Modems

Passing information between computers is, if you think about it, quite mundane. Visit any office with more than one machine in it and, at the very least, you will find the computer users handing each other disks of files etc for use on each other's machines. One step up from this is to link the machines by a suitable cable and have the information passed along that. This process is called networking and, with the right set-up, can be used to link several machines together even in different rooms.

More ambitious users regularly send each other information over the phone lines – to do this requires a modem.

The modem is best thought of as a black box which can transmit and receive digital signals of a predetermined type. The modem need have no understanding of what it is that it is controlling. In principal a modem sends a message to another modem, establishes which machine is to be doing the sending and which is to be doing the receiving, the speed (or baud rate) it will happen at, a declaration of the size of file or files to be sent and a check that the information has been correctly received.

Faster modems cost more money but, because they are faster, you need spend less time on the phone thus saving money. I'll leave you to your own economics calculations. One important point though is that no matter how fast you can receive or send data you can't do it any faster than the machine at the other end of the line!

With the process outlined above in operation there is little need for the users to be around and in the case of Bulletin Boards they rarely are. A Bulletin Board is a computer with hard disk attached that is connected with a modem. Anyone can ring up and *download* whatever takes their fancy. As the process can be somewhat slow and hence expensive most BBS have a comprehensive menu system which can be downloaded first to inspect so that the time spent actually connected across the phone system is reduced to a minimum. In addition, much that they contain is kept in a compressed format.

Modems will typically plug into the RS232 serial port.

Fax Machines

The fax (or facsimile) machine has become the business accessory of the 1990s. It works in a manner similar to a photocopier except that you do the copying at one end of the phone line and the print out occurs at the other. It has an advantage over the phone in that if the person you are sending a message to is out the message still gets through. Whether they do anything about it is a different matter. And it scores over the post in being instantaneous; handy within the country and essential when transmitting to overseas. Also like the postal service there is the problem of *junk* faxes. That's life I guess.

Computer users, who tend to be at the forefront when it comes to embracing any new technology, have been using faxes for a while now and the standard process seems to be along these lines:

1   Wordprocess/DeskTop Publish a document

2   Print it out

3   Fax it

The whole process is rather cumbersome and wasteful. What's happening is a digital message is being output to paper and then scanned to convert it back into another digital format before being sent down the telephone line. Surely there must be a way of cutting out the middle man and letting the computer send the message directly? There is and it's simply a means of connecting the computer to the phone lines via the right hardware. The hardware in question is a fax modem which at one end plugs into the computer and at the other into the phone line.

CD-ROM

Everyone knows what CDs are – they're the expensive alternative to the old hiss and scratch vinyl LPs. It's not the end of the story though because the technology that makes CDs so suitable for recording sound can be applied to many other areas. All that glorious sound on CD is recorded in digital format – ie as a series of zeros and ones – just like on a computer disk. In practice this means that any digital information can be stored on a CD as long as it is written in a format that can be understood.

CD technology on the computer has been a long time in coming or, put another way, it's been around for quite a while but has taken quite a while to catch on.

The main disadvantage of the system is that while CDs can be used to store huge amounts of information (and I mean huge – 500 floppy disks worth is typical) that information can only ever be read; hence the ROM or Read Only Memory part of the name. There's no way the contents of a CD can be altered. For computer users used to tinkering with the look, feel and lay-out of everything they can get their hands on this can be a bit of a drawback. On the plus side the CD can be used to store great libraries of information and it is as a library that they are most popular. CD-ROMs can be purchased with vast stores of pictures for use in art packages or DTP programs or for video effects. Libraries of fonts can be stored on them not to mention there use as a storage for sound.

Apart from all your standard hi-fi CDs which can be played via your computer, you can also buy libraries of sample and sound effects for use within music programs. It is relatively straightforward to put your Pink Floyd CD into the CD-ROM drive, select the segment of sound you want to use and use it as a sound effect in your own software.

CD^{32}

The CD^{32} is the A1200's sibling games console. It consists of a hand-held button pad for controlling games, a CD games player and the cables to link this up with your TV or monitor. It is designed around the same chips that form the heart of the A1200. As a consequence anything the CD^{32} can do the A1200 can do as well.

Many A1200 owners will be keen to get their hands on this new games playing technology and this will be possible through a specialist expansion for the A1200. As the computer already has the processing power, all that is required is a plug-in CD drive. This fits via the trap-door underneath the machine and means that it can't be used in conjunction with an accelerator card or RAM upgrade. An upgrade to Workbench and Kickstart 3.1 is also needed which, if you don't have already, is suppplied with the interface. Workbench 3.1 is merely a replacement for the previous Workbench3.0 disk but Kickstart 3.1 comes on a ROM which means unplugging the old ROM chip and replacing it with the more up to date version.

Scanners

If art packages or desktop publishing come high on your list of activities then a scanner might be worth considering. A scanner is a mechanical device for converting pictures into a digital format that the A1200 can recognise and display. It works a bit like a digitiser/camcorder combination but operates on flat pictures such as photos or illustrations. As ever you get what you pay for, but the cheapest hand-held models will be perfectly acceptable for most home uses. A scanner usually plugs into the computer's parallel port and comes supplied with software to help you achieve good results. All you, the user, have to do is slowly drag the scanner over the image you want to capture. Scanners are usually supplied with some rudimentary (and in some cases quite sophisticated) software for "image processing". Typically this will allow you to adjust the colour settings, rotate all or part of the image and make a host of other refinements. These are often duplicated by the graphics package you are going to load the image into so find out which does the job best.

What you get out depends on what you put in. The better the image being scanned the higher quality the end result. If you're using a mono scanner then it will get best results from black and white originals. If you are planning on cropping the picture then do this before you scan. This doen't mean a pair of scissors – just cover over those unwanted areas with white card. This will reduce the size (in RAM) of your final image and let you use a higher resolution scan.

What you do with the finished image is entirely up to you. It can be loaded into a paint package and retouched – who said the camera never lies? – or used as part of a page design in a desktop publishing program. Wherever you can use pictures, you can use a scanner.

Machine Chatter

For many people the A1200 is a computer to use at home and is used in isolation. Should data be swapped with another machine them this is usually another Amiga somewhere else.

However, the A1200 has many serious applications, particularly in the graphics field and this inevitably means transferring information from it to another type of machine. Other users will have access to computers at work – typically IBM PC compatible machines or Apple Macintoshes – and wish to continue work at home on certain projects.

In its raw state the A1200 is incapable of running programs designed to run on other machines in the same way that other machines can't run Amiga software. Information can still be passed between alien systems though, if the files are of a format that both machines can understand.

The most famous universal file type is ASCII text. Just about every wordprocessor available has the facility to read or export text in this format.

As a format it is decidely *raw*. This means that all the information that is normally part of a wordprocessor file governing text styles, fonts usage, layout details and so on have been stripped out. All that remains is the words and one or two hidden *codes* like the end-of-line instructions.

The advantage is not just the ability to pass text between different systems but also between pieces of software on the same machine. A typical example of this is where a wordprocessor is used to write an article and the text is then ported to a DTP package so the layout can be designed and pictures incorporated. DTP packages are usually equipped to accept text from a variety of wordprocessors but ASCII is one option that is always included. Which is why almost any wordprocessor can be used to write with.

With other file types life isn't quite so easy. Graphics files are a typical example of this – there is no one standard file type to be used, there are several. So when porting files between different systems the first task is to establish which file types they both recognise. To send a photograph scanned on an Amiga to be used in the Macintosh desktop publisher QuarkXPress means using the TIFF file type but if the image is to be "touched up", say in Adobe Photoshop, first then this can be expanded to include GIF and even the Amiga's own IFF/ILBM format. Where there's a will there's a way. Even if the two pieces of software you are using don't share any file types then the situation can often be saved by using a file translator which converts files of one type to another.

Music files on different machines can also be swapped. The most popular source is the Atari ST which uses the "Tracker" format. Databases are usually capable of exporting and importing data in the raw CSV (Comma Separated Variable) format.

With all the file transfer methods mentioned above it is wise to make sure that, if you are transferring data on floppy disks, you use a disk format that both machines can understand. More often than not this will be the 720K PC disk format.

One Step Further

There is a way in which software from one computer can run on a different machine and that's by using an *emulator*. This is a piece of software that makes its host machine capable of behaving as though it were a different computer. Thus a Mac-emulator for the A1200 will make it capable of using software written for the Apple Macintosh. There are, however, several drawbacks with this:

• The emulator itself often uses up a lot of RAM leaving little left for running any applications.

• Using software on an emulator tends to be much slower than using it on the original machine as there is much more processing involved. This may not be particularly apparent with a wordprocessor but with anything else it can be a severe handicap.

• It is still illegal to copy software. Therefore, if you want to use Mac software on your Amiga's emulator you'll have to buy your own copies.

Speed is the biggest issue here and one way that manufacturers have tried to get round this is by building specialist hardware add-ons that perform much of the processing – it's almost like adding another computer to your Amiga. The disadvantage this time is the cost and the choice at this stage is often between the hardware upgrade and a new machine.

Warning

These things tend to escalate. Let's say for example you buy yourself a scanner. This lets you use lots of extra pictures in your DTP package. Unfortunately these increase the file size of eveything you produce so you really need a hard disk. The next problem you encounter is that manipulating large files slows the A1200 down so you decide to buy an accelerator; while you're at it you might as well throw in some extra RAM. It seems a shame to have all this kit and not be able to see what you are producing so a larger monitor is next on the shopping list... and so it goes on.

Insider Guide #17: Crossing between DOSs.

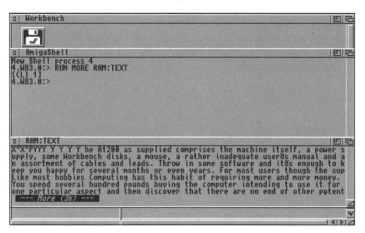

Transferring files between computer systems can be something of a headache. The first thing to check is whether the systems use a common file type. ASCII is a universal standard for text files and all word-processors should be able to import a file in this format. However, not all wps can export files in this format (if they can there is usually a Save as ASCII option or something similar).

A file from a wordprocessor of this nature is far from useless and is normally just a process of stripping out large sections of code at the start and end of the file which only make sense to the original word-processor. One or two symbols may not match between systems but, again, there is a quick solution. Most wordprocessors have a "Search and Replace" or "Find" option which allows all instances of one or more symbols to be replaced or removed.

14

The A1200 is famed as a graphics machine. To get the most from it, then, you need the right display...

```
IControl Preferences                          [回][回]
                                  Coercion
         Screen Drag          Avoid Flicker:  [✓]
      [ ] ⇧ (SHIFT)          Preserve Colors: [✓]
      [ ] CTRL
      [ ] ALT                   Miscellaneous
      [✓] A (LEFT AMIGA)     Screen Menu Snap:   [✓]
                            Text Gadget Filter:  [✓]
                               Mode Promotion:   [ ]
   [  Save  ]        [   Use   ]        [  Cancel  ]
```

*O*ne of the joys of the A1200 is that its design allows it to be plugged straight into the back of your television set. You don't need to spend any more money on a specialist computer monitor. This is one of the reasons that the machine has been so sucessful as a home computer – you get all that computing power at a premium price.

The drawbacks of this approach are that you will inevitably find occasions when someone else wants to watch TV at exactly the same time as you want to sit down to a spot of computing. And even if this conflict doesn't arise you will still find that you encounter shortcomings with the screen image on the TV screen. For anything other than games it isn't really good enough. Not only that, a TV doesn't allow you to display those AGA screen modes that sets the A1200 aside from earlier Amigas and most other computers as well. This shouldn't come as any surprise – TVs were designed to accept a TV signal and computer monitors to display computer images, the two aren't the same. One further bonus in using a monitor is that most are equipped with a speaker on either side of the screen allowing you to experiment with stereo sound of a quality higher than most TV sets will allow.

How it all Works

Computer monitors work in much the same way as a TV screen. Electrons are fired by a cathode ray gun at phosphor dots. When they hit the dots the dots glow; in a colour monitor these dots are of red, green and blue (RGB) and there is a separate ray gun for each colour. The screen image is composed entirely of glowing dots of red, green and blue which, as a whole, form the image you want to see. The distance between dots on a TV screen – the dot pitch – is about 0.6mm. On a computer screen it is 0.4mm or less which is why you get a sharper picture.

Multisyncs

A standard computer monitor will allow you to view everything that the TV screen will let you see, only with much greater clarity. However, to use the full capabilities of the AGA graphics chip set, you will need a multisync (or at least a dual sync) monitor. These are even more expensive than standard monitors but, if you're seriously into graphics then you have little option. Ordinarily the Amiga's screen output is of a specific frequency – in the 15kHz range – which a standard monitor can accept but the new AGA modes work at about double that figure. To view these requires a monitor capable of coping with that input. A multisync, which can accept all manner of screen frequencies is one option, a dual sync – which can cope with just the top, narrow, frequency ranges – is the other. The dual sync option is generally cheaper and should be enough for most uses as long as you are happy that you won't want to display screen modes from yet further frequencies.

There are no end of multisync and dual sync monitors to choose from at a wide variety of prices. Commodore themselves supply a range of dual sync monitors that work at both the required frequencies.

Monitor Types

Having chosen a monitor the appropriate choice needs to be made via the Extras disk Preferences option. If, for example, you have chosen an A2024 monitor then the appropri-

Insider Guide #20: Choosing display modes

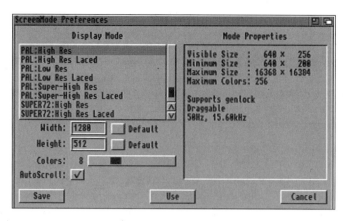

*Open the ScreenMode utility from the Preferences directory on the
Extras disk. The Display options you have available are listed on the
right. In turn select the various options and then click on "Use" to see
their effect.*

*Toggle the Default buttons so that you can enter a custom screen
size. Choose figures that are larger than the "Visible Size" listed under
"Mode Properties". Now select Use.*

*The Workbench window is now larger than can be accommodated on
the screen. To access the parts that others cannot reach move the
mouse of the righthand edge or bottom of the screen and the display
will follow. Screens can also be configured down to a minimum size
that doesn't use the entire available area.*

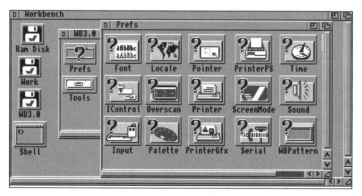

ate screen mode needs to be selected from the Monitors subdirectory of the Devices directory on the Storage disk.

Display Modes

Choose the screen mode you need and drag it into the Devs/Monitors directory on your boot-up disk. Unless you are in the habit of swapping between different types of monitors or have a multisync monitor there should only ever be the one driver in this directory.

With the appropriate monitor driver installed, open the Preferences directory on the Extras disk. The ScreenMode program allows you to make your choices about the screen appearance. On the left is a table of the Display Modes available to you. These include the six default settings (in the UK) for PAL monitors. A PAL monitor is anyone which operates at the same frequencies as a television. In the United States the equivalent is NTSC – televsions there run at subtly different frequencies.

Highlight any one of the monitor options and the properties of that screen mode will be displayed in the righthand window. I am assuming that, like me, you have a PAL monitor to play around with. If this isn't the case then some of the settings I mention will be different for your monitor but in any case I have included them in Table 14.1.

Mode Properties

The mode properties are concerned with the size of the screen display and the number of colours available for use. The PAL monitor options offer three differing types of display: 1280 x 256, 320 x 256 and 640 x 256. The first figure represents the width of the visible screen in numbers of pixels and the second is its height. The default option is 640 x 256 pixels. (Pixels, if you remember are picture elements; those blocks that go to make up the total screen image. They are not the same as the phosphor dots mentioned earlier.)

Choose the Super-High Res option, click on "Use" and then watch as your screen is transformed. The items on the Workbench screen suddenly seem very much smaller. Although each opened window is using as many pixels to describe it as it was before there are now many more pixels on the screen, the overall effect being to create more space on the Workbench. It is twice the previous total area.

Display Mode	VisSize	MinSize	MaxSize	MCols	ECS	gen	drag	Hz
A2024:10Hz	1024x1024	1024x1024	16368x16384	4	–	N	Y	50, 15.6k
A2024:15Hz	1024x1024	1024x1024	16368x16384	4	–	N	Y	50, 15.6k
DBLNTSC:High Res	640x200	640x200	16368x16384	256	-	N	Y	58, 27.66k
DBLNTSC:High Res Laced	640x800	640x200	16368x16384	256	req	N	Y	58, 27.66k
DBLNTSC:High Res No Flicker	640x400	640x200	16368x16384	256	req	N	Y	58, 27.66k
DBLNTSC:Low Res	320x200	640x200	16368x16384	256	-	N	Y	58, 27.66k
DBLNTSC:Low Res Laced	320x800	640x200	16368x16384	256	req	N	Y	58, 27.66k
DBLNTSC:Low Res No Flicker	320x400	640x200	16368x16384	256	req	N	Y	58, 27.66k
DBLPAL:High Res	640x256	640x200	16368x16384	256	-	N	Y	48, 27.50k
DBLPAL:High Res Laced	640x1024	640x200	16368x16384	256	req	N	Y	48, 27.50k
DBLPAL:High Res No Flicker	640x512	640x200	16368x16384	256	req	N	Y	48, 27.50k
DBLPAL:Low Res	320x256	640x200	16368x16384	256	-	N	Y	48, 27.50k
DBLPAL:Low Res Laced	320x1024	640x200	16368x16384	256	req	N	Y	48, 27.50k
DBLPAL:Low Res No Flicker	320x512	640x200	16368x16384	256	req	N	Y	48, 27.50k
EURO:36Hz High Res	640x200	640x200	16368x16384	256	req	N	Y	73, 15.76k
EURO:36Hz High Res Laced	640x200	640x400	16368x16384	256	req	N	Y	73, 15.76k
EURO:36Hz Low Res	320x200	640x200	16368x16384	256	req	N	Y	73, 15.76k
EURO:36Hz Low Res Laced	320x400	640x200	16368x16384	256	req	N	Y	73, 15.76k
EURO:36Hz Super-High Res	1280x200	640x200	16368x16384	256	req	N	Y	73, 15.76k
EURO:36Hz Super-High Res Lac	1280x400	640x200	16368x16384	256	req	N	Y	73, 15.76k

Table 14.1. Monitor Specifications.

EURO:72Hz:Productivity	640x400	640x200	16368x16384	256	req	N	Y	70, 31.43k
EURO:72Hz:Productivity Laced	640x800	640x200	16368x16384	256	req	N	Y	70, 31.43k
MULTISCAN:Productivity	640x480	640x200	16368x16384	256	req	N	Y	58, 29.29k
MULTISCAN:Productivity Laced	640x960	640x200	16368x16384	256	req	N	Y	58, 29.29k
NTSC:High Res	640x200	640x200	16368x16384	256	-	Y	Y	60, 15.72k
NTSC:High Res Laced	640x400	640x200	16368x16384	256	-	Y	Y	60, 15.72k
NTSC:Low Res	320x200	640x200	16368x16384	256	-	Y	Y	60, 15.72k
NTSC:Low Res Laced	320x400	640x200	16368x16384	256	-	Y	Y	60, 15.72k
NTSC:Super-High Res	1280x200	640x200	16368x16384	256	req	Y	Y	60, 15.72k
NTSC:Super-High Res Laced	1280x400	640x200	16368x16384	256	req	Y	Y	60, 15.72k
PAL:1280 x 256	1280x256	640x200	16368x16384	256	req	Y	Y	50, 15.6k
PAL:1280 x 512 Interlaced	1280x512	640x200	16368x16384	256	req	Y	Y	50, 15.6k
PAL:320 x 256	320x256	640x200	16368x16384	256	-	Y	Y	50, 15.6k
PAL:320 x 512 Interlaced	320x512	640x200	16368x16384	256	-	Y	Y	50, 15.6k
PAL:640 x 256	640x256	640x200	16368x16384	256	-	Y	Y	50, 15.6k
PAL:640 x 512 Interlaced	640x512	640x200	16368x16384	256	-	Y	Y	50, 15.6k
SUPER72:High Res	400x300	640x200	16368x16384	256	req	N	Y	72, 24.62k
SUPER72:High Res Laced	400x600	640x200	16368x16384	256	req	N	Y	72, 24.62k
SUPER72:Super-High Res	800x300	640x200	16368x16384	256	req	N	Y	72, 24.62k
SUPER72:Super-High Res Laced	800x600	640x200	16368x16384	256	req	N	Y	72, 24.62k

Table 14.1 continued. Monitor Specifications.

If you are accustomed to having numerous windows open at once – something which is most likely to happen if you have extra RAM and are therefore capable of multitasking to a much greater degree – then this could be the mode for you.

Having selected your chosen mode you can now modify it for your own personal use. Beneath the righthand Display Modes windows are the gadgets for selecting screen size for the mode you have chosen. Clicking on the default buttons allows new figures to be inserted in the width and height boxes. You can type in virtually any figures you like here as long as they are no smaller than the miminum size and no larger than the maximum size options shown in the Mode Properties. Using the 640 x 256 option, for example, let's try figures of 1280 wide by 512 high. Clicking on "Use" presents the familiar Workbench screen but with no apparent righthand or bottom edges. Now try moving the mouse off the bottom or the right of the screen and what happens is that the whole screen scrolls to reveal even more screen. One further option here is the Autoscroll gadget. If this isn't ticked (checked) then the ability to move off the screen is disabled. I'm not sure why you would ever want to do this. The net effect of all this is that the screen can be customised so that the items on it are reduced in size and/or so that the screen itself is of a different size.

IControl

If you do use a screen larger than fits onto the screen you will still want to use the menu options at the top-left of the screen even when working elsewhere on the screen. That is possible because the option that sets this is, by default, set to "on". The IControl preferences utility has an option headed "Screen Menu Snap" which does just this.

Also inside this utility are options which relate to the Productivity modes found on some multiscan monitors. When using several screens on one of these monitors the front screen is the only one likely to have the optimum display quality. To try and improve the picture quality on the lower screens the "Avoid Flicker", and "Preserve Colors" options are toggled on. If the results aren't to your liking you might try resetting them.

The screen drag option merely controls how a screen can be dragged. You can drag the title bar or by clicking anywhere on the screen and holding down the chosen key (Shift, Ctrl, Alt or Left-Amiga).

More Colours

The number of colours available can also be altered. By default this is just four but this can be adjusted in most screen modes up to 256. This is the maximum number that can be displayed on a Workbench screen at any one time but if you are using a graphics package which has its own screen then you will need to look within the options of that program to alter its capabilities.

Now if you're really sharp you may remember playing round with the Preference settings in the Palette utility. There, on the screen, is a colour wheel with 256 different colours showing how you can customise the colours of the desktop. How can 256 colours be displayed here and not normally?

The answer is that the Palette window doesn't normally open onto a Workbench screen. Select a four-colour option from the screen modes options and then open the Palette window. You will see that it can't be moved around like any other window but that it sits on its own screen.

However, if you choose 256 colours in the Screen Modes utility and now open the Palette window you will find that it has a normal Workbench window of its own. Very cunning!

Catch 22

By default the A1200 expects to see one specific kind of monitor. To use anything different requires changing the monitor driver. However, to change the monitor driver requires being able to see what you are doing...

If you are only ever going to use your A1200 with a non-standard monitor you need to get your dealer to change the preferences for you before you leave the shop or, more probably, you need to find a TV or similar to perform this operation on. You must have one lying around somewhere.

Lost Memory

So why not use the largest possible screen size in as many colours as are available? Each enhancement you make to the appearance of the screen costs more in terms of memory. As you add to the number of available colours and the area of the screen the available memory figure at the top of the Workbench screen decreases. It's a good idea to keep an eye on this figure during the course of your computing. Should you need to free up some extra memory for a particulalrly RAM-hungry operation then this can be one useful source. Getting by with just two colours, black and grey, certainly isn't pretty but if it gets the job done it can't be all bad.

Some applications regularly use almost all your available RAM – DTP packages are common culprits – and if you can get by in a simpler screen mode then do so.

Interlacing

Pretty well every screen mode has an accompanying mode called "Laced". Interlacing is a method of fitting more onto the screen than should normally be possible given the constraints of the hardware involved.

In normal, non-laced, modes the information on screen is updated at between 50 and 70 times a second, fast enough to deceive the eye into seeing a static or smoothly moving image. Interlacing effectively crams twice as many horizontal lines onto the screen by displaying each line alternately. Thus lines 1, 3, 5, 7 etc are shown followed by lines 2, 4, 6, 8 and so on. The net result is a larger screen area but the cost is the flickering image that results. If this is one area you wish to explore then enquire about the costs of a "flicker-fixer", a little hardware add-on which will do just what its name suggests.

Graphics Cards

As they can display far more colours than the unexpanded A1200, Amigas that are fitted with 24-bit graphics cards are also supplied with their own custom screen modes. This sort of add-on is for the dedicated graphics user and a multisync monitor is essential – there's no point playing round with all those extra colours if you can't see them!

Mode Properties

The information in the Mode Properties window includes "requires ECS" and "draggable" appended to some of the screen modes. Neither criterion need worry us. ECS is the Enhanced Chip Set which is standard in the A1200 and draggable means that individual screens – such as the Workbench screen – can be dragged by mouse in the manner we are accustomed to.

The Visible Size is that which can be viewed at any one time. The Minimum Size is just that. If you try and enter a lower figure the default minimum will be used instead.

15

A hard disk drive is *the* A1200 dream accessory. Fitting it and setting it up doesn't have to be a nightmare...

*O*nce you've been using your Amiga for a while you'll become aware of certain shortcomings and will start to think of the many different ways in which your set-up can be improved.

The two most popular improvements involve expanding the size of the memory and adding a hard drive. A hard drive is viewed by many to be such an essential part of the modern computer that few other than the cheapest home computers (such as the Amiga A1200) are sold without them. This does offer us quite an advantage though. Machines that are sold with a hard drive fitted don't always give you the choice of what size you would prefer – you get what you're given and that's it.

Hard Drive Facts

If you've become used to juggling with several disks whenever you want to perform even the simplest of actions on your machine then the thought may have occurred to you "Wouldn't it be easier if these disks could hold more data?"

If a disk held 40Mb instead of just one then it would be possible to put the contents of both Workbench and Extras disks onto it, a word-processor, some games and all the projects you're working on rather than have to do endless disk swaps. The hard drive is that 40 Megabyte disk and it doesn't have to be 40Mb – it can be as little as 20Mb or as large as several hundred. The only difference is you can't slot it in and out of your machine like a floppy disk. It's a separate entity altogether and normally fits permanently inside your machine. But you can store all your data on it and still have the floppy disk drive available for transferring data to different sources eg from magazine disks.

No IDEa?

Start talking about hard disks and words and phrases like "IDE", "SCSI" and "access speeds" start cropping up all over the place. It doesn't have to be that complicated but, if you really must know, then IDE stands for "Integrated Drive Electronics", SCSI stands for "Small Computer Systems Interface" and access speed is the time taken for information to be retrieved from or written to the hard disk.

There are all sorts of complicated ways of measuring a hard disk's access speed and the more technical magazines periodically run comparisons judged on various criteria. Forget it. Although some appear to be several times faster than others the net result is that the fastest are almost instantaneous in their response whilst the slowest are still so fast that it makes no odds. I'm not aware of there being a hard disk on the market for the A1200 which is so slow as to be a handicap in normal use. Save your money then and don't be lured into buying something which has impressive credentials that make no difference.

The criteria which you should consider are a) can it be used with an Amiga A1200? and b) what size should I get?

How it Works

Take a floppy disk to pieces (but not one you'll ever need again!) and you'll find a thin disk of grey-black plastic. This is the floppy part and it's also the part on which everything is recorded. It's done in much the same way as music is recorded onto a tape cassette. A hard disk is like a stack of these floppy disks all stored together in a hard case. Plug it into your Amiga and suddenly you have 20, 40 or however many Megabytes of extra storage.

Which Hard Disk?

The most complicated technical data I would advise you to study when purchasing a hard drive is your own requirements. Take a look at the disks you normally use: the programs and utilities, the data disks and add up the total in Mbs. This is the minimum size of hard disk that you'll need. In practice having a hard disk provides many freedoms and my own preference is to err on the side of gross excess. Having too large a hard disk means that it takes longer to fill up – something that it will inevitably do. Too small a hard disk and you will find yourself continuously having to make decisions about what goes on it and what doesn't. Save the extra pennies and buy yourself the next bigger one than you thought you would actually need.

A further consideration is that as you use your computer more and more the amount of programs you regularly use will increase. Actually having a hard disk means that the process of exploration is speeded up increasing the rate at which you need a larger hard drive! There are 20Mb disks on the market but I can't imagine any coping with just that – buy a 40 or even 60Mb one if you can.

Having said all this, and having persuaded you to spend more than you would have preferred in buying that slightly bigger disk, you still need to be careful. Hard disks are like magnets for every stray bit of data that goes around. Be incautious and it will fill up faster than you can say "I wish I had a larger hard disk."

The software that goes with a hard drive will supply a running total of the amount of storage space used and that still available. Keep an eye on these totals and try and make sure that you're not saving any old rubbish onto it. If you don't need a file for immediate use then put it somewhere else.

Up and Running

Once the hard drive is installed and set up with all the software that you need you'll never look back. In fact it does become difficult to appreciate how those other Amiga users can cope without one.

The advantage does not just lie in being able to do those many things you were using your Amiga for beforehand without spending hours playing around with floppies. The extra speed and convenience means that new avenues will be opened for exploration and that you will be able to use utilities and functions that you wouldn't have bothered with beforehand.

OK so you've decided you want a hard drive and you've saved up your money – what next? As ever there is a choice. Option One is to take your machine down to the local dealers and to get them to fit, partition and format your hard drive and load everything you need onto it ready for use. Option Two is to do everything yourself. It can be a cheaper option and it's also far more exciting.

Option Two

Any old hard drive won't do so, before you buy, shop around and make sure that the one you intend using will be suitable for the A1200. You need a 2.5 inch IDE drive but it has to be approved for the A1200.

Fitting the beast isn't as difficult as might at first seem but, if you are doing it yourself, it will invalidate your machine warranty should that still apply. This is proven by the stickers that cover the joins in the computer casing – if they're broken your warranty no longer applies. (If you can remove these stickers without breaking them I'll be impressed!) So, if anything goes wrong with the machine, and you take it back to the shop they'll be within their rights to charge for any work done. If this hasn't put you off then there's no stopping you...

You'll need a number of things to help you. Steady hands, screwdrivers, a hard drive plus cradle, connecting cable and installation software. For the latter I have used Commodore's own "HDToolBox" program.

Disclaimer

You should bear in mind that if you fit your own hard drive, you will almost certainly breach your computer's warranty. Do bear this in mind, especially if your A1200 is new. Also do not attempt to undertake this exercise unless you are quite sure what you are going to do. While the process is relatively straightforward neither the publishers of this book, or the author can be held responsible for any damage caused to person or machine.

Fitting the Drive

The first thing to do is to disconnect the machine from the mains and indeed from any other external appliance such as mouse, joystick, monitor, printer, extra floppy drive and so on and then wiat for at least thirty seconds to let any static discharge. Then turn the A1200 over onto its back and undo the screws holding the casing together. I find it quite handy not to throw these away. Carefully slit the warranty seals and now, holding the case together, turn the machine back the right way up again. Easy does it.

Lift the top of the case off and look inside the machine. A hard drive cradle is fitted internally and your unit will bolt into this. Once fitted the top of the case presses against the cradle to prevent it from moving around.

You will need a suitable 3.5inch IDE hard drive with cable, a small crosshead screwdriver and enough patience to do the job with meticulous care. Warning! Fitting a hard drive yourself will invalidate your machine's warranty.

1. Disconnect the machine from everything else: mouse, monitor, printer and, above all else, the power supply.

2. Turn the A1200 upside down and undo the retaining screws.

3. Turn the machine the right way round and lift the top. This requires a little jiggling to free it from the catches at the back of the machine.

4. Disconnect the disk drive LEDs.

5. Slide the keyboard back until it is free of the catches and then place behind the main body of the machine – it should still be connected to your A1200.

6. Fit the hard drive to the cradle if it has not been supplied and plug the hard drive cable into the pins.

7. Fit the hard drive/cradle unit into the main board

8. Reassemble the machine.

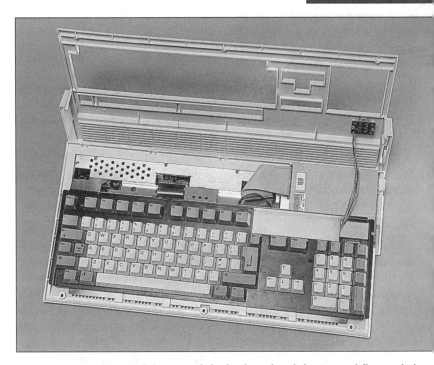

Above: Open the case lid to reveal the keyboard and the internal floppy disk drive in the top lefthand corner.

Below: Remove the keyboard to expose the innards. Disconnect the disk drive LEDs to make access easier.

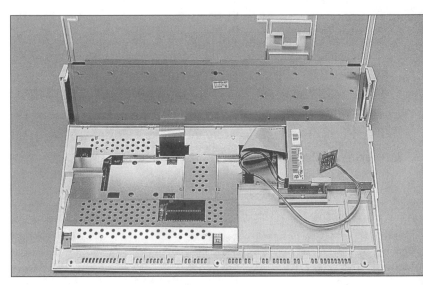

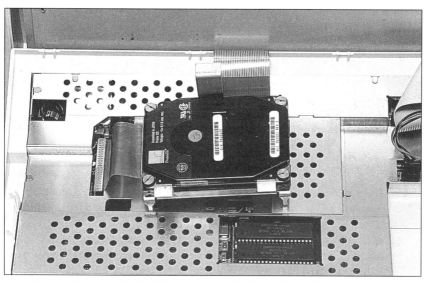

Above: If not supplied with its own cradle, fit the hard disk drive to the A1200's cradle. Position the drive so that the cable ribbon is to the left and plug it into the array of pins. Make sure that pins and holes correspond, do not force anything.

Below: The cradle's feet should fit back into purpose-made sockets. Physical installation is really that easy. Now replace the keyboard and disk drive LEDs. Reassemble the A1200 case and reconnect all external appliances. Insert the Workbench disk and switch on. Physical installation is now complete but the disk now needs to be prepared as a boot disk...

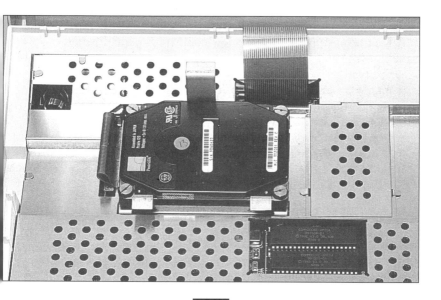

The hard disk is secured in its place, the case has been reassembled and all the add-ons re-attached. Put the Workbench disk into the internal drive and switch on. If all has gone well the machine should boot up as normal but, in addition to the normal floppy drive commotion, there should be an additional, subtler, whirring sound. The A1200 has discovered the hard drive and has powered it up. Like any other disk, the hard drive must be formatted before it is any use but, unlike a floppy disk, there are various additional options to consider.

Partitioning

It is common practice to make the hard drive behave in such a manner that the A1200 thinks it is dealing with two or more component parts – *partitioning* as it's called. The benefits are speed and security. With a physically smaller disk to search the access speeds are improved and, heaven forbid, should something go wrong then the damage will normally be restricted to just one partition. To partition a drive requires using appropriate software. I used "HDToolBox" and will refer to that but there may well be other alternatives that you wish to try.

HDToolBox

Put the HDToolBox disk in the internal drive and launch the program. The first thing that happens is the software informs you that your IDE drive is a SCSI device. Don't worry it's just telling lies. Click on the "Change Drive Type" button which brings up another window confirming your drive as a SCSI (still lying) and presenting you with a further option of "Define new drive type". Click on that and yet another window is revealed. This contains a bewildering array of options and technical detail but the only one that interests us is the "Read Configuration From Drive" option. Rather than having to read all manner of technical data ourselves this just loads the info from the hard disk itself and gets in with it. Click on "Continue" in the system request box this produces, and then on "OK". This returns us to the previous window where another "OK" takes us back to the starting window.

All that this has done is name the drive and make the information available to HDToolBox.

The next step is to partition the hard drive. This disk I have been using is only 20Mb (I stole it from an A600) so I have just split it into two sections but three is probably more useful. You will want one partition to put the routine Workbench stuff on and 6Mb should be enough for that.

My suggestion is to split the rest of the disk into two roughly equal partitions. Try and think about what you are going to put in each partition. Ideally you want to organise things so that when a program is up and running it isn't using three separate partitions all at once but restricts its searching to just the one. Otherwise any speed advantages are negated. So, for example, if you put a DTP package into one partition then you will want the fonts there, any clipart files and plenty of space to store any finished work. It isn't a bad idea to sit down with pen and paper and work out what is going to go where before you partition. Re-partitioning a hard disk afterwards is a pain to say the least.

Having decided what size partitions you are going to use then click on the "Partition Drive" option. This displays yet another window and it is here that you determine how many and how large the partitions are to be. The large horizontal bar depicts the storage space on the hard disk and the little arrowhead beneath it can be moved back and forth to select a suitable size for each partition. Drag it left until the "Size" reading states "6 Meg". Now click in the "Partition Device Name" window and type in a suitable name for that partition – such as "WB3.0" – and then click on the "Bootable?" option to display "Yes". Repeat the process for any subsequent partitions except for the "Bootable?" part, and then click on "OK". This returns you to the opening window where you can now click on the "Save Changes to Drive" option.

Loading WB3

You should now have on the Workbench screen additional disk icons similar to those used for a disk in the floppy drive or the Ram Disk – one for each partition. And, like any unformatted floppy disk, they may well be indicated as being "BAD". Select one partition and then use the Format option from the Workbench "Icons" menu. Decide now whether or not you want the Trashcan and select the "Fast File System" option. You will need to repeat the name you have chosen for the partition as Workbench has a habit of wanting to call everything "Empty". Then click on the "Format" option and sit back, confirm several times that this is what you want to do (the A1200 has been designed to make sure that you don't do this sort of thing by accident) and wait for it to be done.

Allow anything up to a minute per Megabyte for the formatting to be done – a graphical display will tell you how things are progressing.

Having done it with one partition you can now do it with all the others. Once you have finished you should have a Workbench screen with several disk icons displayed: one for the Workbench disk in the internal disk drive; one for the Ram Disk; one for each hard drive partition; and one for each of any RAD disks you may have included in your set-up.

Almost There...

The final step is to place all the Workbench information onto the bootable partition of the hard drive. This isn't just from the Workbench disk but all the others such as Extras, Storage and so on. The quickest way to do this is with the COPY command in either the Shell or via the "Execute Command..." option. To copy Workbench from a disk in the internal drive to a partition called "WB3.0" use:

```
COPY DF0:#? WB3.0: ALL CLONE
```

The CLONE option ensures that all the files copied across retain their original date stamps and any filenotes that have been appended. Repeat the process with the Extras disk. One thing that you will notice happening when you do this is that certain parts of the Workbench and Extras disk appear to merge together. Each disk has its own "System" directory for example but on the hard drive there is only one and this contains the content of both previous "System" directories.

This has all been carefully planned by Commodore when the original five disks were compiled. Ideally everything on the Workbench and the Extras disk would have been squeezed onto the one disk but this simply wasn't feasible. So the material on the two disks was arranged so that the Extras disk contains all the information that is only needed on an occasional basis. However, when the two disks are put together onto one hard drive partition all that flexibility is available at once.

A similar procedure to above is called for when copying the Fonts, Storage and Locale disks onto the hard drive. But, as we don't want their information in the root directory they should be copied into directories that bear their names:

```
COPY DF0:#? WB3.0:FONTS ALL CLONE

COPY DF0:#? WB3.0:STORAGE ALL CLONE
```

COPY DF0:#? WB3.0:LOCALE ALL CLONE

Suitably set-up the Workbench partition now has all that it is going to need – for the time being at least. Empty the internal drive and then perform a soft reboot.

(If your Workbench is booting off a RAD disk then you will have to switch the machine off, wait a few seconds and then switch on again. This time it should boot up from the hard drive. If you have RAD disks included as part of your startup process then now is as good a time as any to get rid of them. You can use the hard drive in exactly the same way and you will find the extra RAM that this liberates will be invaluable.)

Now when you double-click on the WB3.0 icon (or whatever else you have called it) all the files should be there to see. Most of them will be piled on top of each other but this can be quickly rectified by successively choosing the "Select Contents", "Clean Up" and "Snapshot" options from the Workbench menus or by using the following hot-key combinations: <Amiga><A>, <Amiga><.> and <Amiga><S>.

16

In Chapter 15 we looked at installing a hard drive. Having done that we ask "What's changed?"

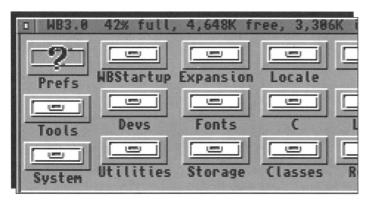

*N*ow that your hard disk is installed, every time you switch on the A1200 the machine will boot up from the hard drive. This, as you will find to your pleasure, is considerably quicker than doing the same from floppy disk. With no need to keep a Workbench disk lying around, the internal floppy drive can be used without the previous endless disk swapping hassles.

The way the Startup-Sequence has been written you do not need to rewrite any of it for the machine to understand that it is booting Workbench from a hard drive. A useful part of the Startup-Sequence is the setting of default paths for Tools and Tools/Commodities which are normally found on the Extras disk. Now if you type , say, CALCULATOR into the Shell the calculator appears on screen rather than the previous "Unknown command" message.

Loading Up

The next step is to start copying your most-needed programs onto the other partition(s) on the hard drive. This requires a bit of advanced planning. The best way of doing it is to create a directory for each application.

Let's assume you have a wordprocessor called "Scrawl". Create a directory of that name and then copy across all the files that you will need for its use: the Scrawl application itself, any dictionary that comes with it, the files you are working on and anything else that appears to be hanging around that you think might come in handy. The great advantage of the hard drive is that this directory can be, and often is, much bigger than could previously be squeezed onto the one floppy disk. If the Scrawl application previously booted from its own disk then it may have access to its own tools. Thus the C: directory on that floppy disk may well contain commands that aren't on your Workbench partition and which Scrawl needs to run properly. The best course of action is to use the "Show >> All Files" option on the Workbench Window menu and have a good root round to see if there is anything else you need.

If there are files missing that the program needs then it will soon complain about it saying "Can't open...". Find the file it is looking for and copy it to your hard drive. The second difficulty that you can encounter is that a System Request continually prompts you to "Please insert volume..." It does so because its Default Tool setting includes the name of a disk. Click on the program in question and then open its "Information" window. Rewrite the Default Tool setting to suit your hard drive partition. If these options fail to get the program running smoothly from the hard disk check that there isn't a special hard disk install utility to go with the program. If there isn't then the chances are that the program won't run from a hard drive. Not all programs will, but all commercial ones should. If in doubt check with the manufacturers.

Floppy Boots

Although you can now boot up from the hard drive and will tend to do so most of the time there are occasions when you might want to boot from a floppy disk instead. The A1200 set-up allows you to do just that. If it finds a bootable disk in the internal drive on boot-up then the A1200 will use that by default. This can be very handy when you have a program that doesn't want to use

Workbench – games in particular. The other occasion when this could be useful is in the awful eventuality of something nasty going wrong with the hard drive. Just think about it – if the A1200 kept trying to boot up from a broken hard drive then you'd really be in trouble.

Hard Games

One thing you will find is that some applications, games in particular, can't be copied across onto the hard drive. This is because of the way in which they have been protected. In an effort to prevent software piracy – the illegal copying and selling of their software – many games manufacturers make a habit of including software protection that prevents their programs from being copied. In practice these methods are never foolproof but they do deter casual piracy.

However, as most games need to take over the whole machine and don't want anything to do with Workbench, you will normally need to boot from the main games disk anyway and that means booting from the floppy drive. However, if there are several disks involved in the game – as there often are – these extra disks can often be copied to your hard drive without any difficulty.

Utility Help

One or two handy utilities will help enormously with the day to day running of your hard disk. An "application launcher" is used to load programs without having to hunt through the relevant directories. This is particularly useful if you have a large hard disk containing a lot of applications.

The "All is not Lost" chapter contains an explanation of how saved files can become fragmented while still appearing, on the Workbench, as complete units. This process takes rather longer to become a problem on a hard drive but, when it does, it can slow down its operation quite considerably. One way round the problem is to backup the hard disk partition, reformat it and then load the files back onto it. This is certainly effective although a little slow and you may choose to buy a separate "defragmentor" utility instead which handles these details for you.

Another handy utility is a file finder. The hard drive quickly becomes home to hundreds, thousands even, of files and there are occasions when you need to find a particular file in a hurry – now which directory did I put it in? The answer is to employ a utility to do the job for you. It asks you to enter the file name your'e looking for and then sifts through as many hard drive partitions as you care to choose, searching for all instances of files of that name. These are then listed out alongside their path names.

With a hard disk the dangers of virus attack becomes more acute as, at any one time, you have far more files that are exposed. Keeping exposure to dubious software sources down to a minimum will reduce the risks but the only surefire way of protecting your set-up is to include a virus checker in the startup sequence. This will ensure that everytime a new disk is placed in the internal drive – or any other floppy that you might have, for that matter – that disk is scanned to make sure it isn't carrying a virus. Inevitably this slows down the whole process a little but the few seconds you have to wait each time will more than repay themselves should you prevent just one infection. Whatever utilities you buy, though, put a back-up program at the top of the list.

Beware of...

The easiest way to damage your hard drive is to drop it, so don't. You should always be careful when moving computer equipment around but once you have a hard drive fitted only ever do it when the machine is switched off. The "heads" that read the data from the hard drive hover perilously close to the surfaces of the drive when it is in operation and a sudden jolt can make head and disk surface come into contact. Ouch. The effect usually involves the loss of data. But when a hard drive is switched off the heads are parked away from the danger zone and the risks reduced. Don't take that to mean you can throw it around – it's still a delicate device.

They may be robust units but damage to them can mean the loss of weeks, months even, of sweat and toil. If you're using your A1200 for business uses that might not just be inconvenient, it's going to be expensive as well. You need to make a regular back-up as an exercise in damage limitation.

The other danger is doing something daft like resetting the A1200 while the hard drive is in operation – this will inevitably wipe some data but only in the partition that is being accessed.

Insider Guide #19: Getting software to run from a hard disk.

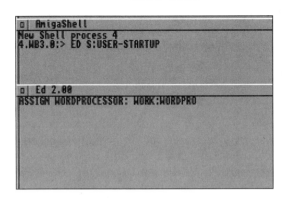

Copy the software you wish to use to the Work: partition of the hard disk. Try and use it – if it works then great. if it doesn't then use this checklist:

1. Is there a hard drive install program specifically for that piece of software? If so then use it.

2. Does the program send out error messages stating that certain obscure files could not be found? If so locate each file mentioned from the original software disks and copy them into the equivalent directories on the Workbench partition of the hard disk.

3. Does the program request the original software disk? eg:

Please insert Wordprocessor disk

If so, the program has been written to look for that disk as part of its normal use. However the program can be conned into thinking it has found the disk by ASSIGNing it to the directory on the hard disk where you have placed it.

Confused? Imagine the program sends out a

Please insert Wordprocessor disk

message. Make a note of where you have stored the program on the hard disk. For example in the "Work:WordPro" directory. Create an ED file

ED S:USER-STARTUP

then in the newly created file (or at the end of an existing file of that name) type:

ASSIGN WORDPROCESSOR: WORK:WORDPRO

Save the file and reboot the machine. Now, every time the program wants to look at the Wordprocessor disk AmigaDOS redirects its search to the appropriate directory on the hard disk.

If you start moving programs around on your hard disk don't forget that you may have to rewrite the User-Startup file accordingly.

No Parking

When a hard drive is switched off it is safest for the heads to be "parked" away from the disk surface. This reduces the risks of damage should the unit be jolted in transit etc. This is not something that users of modern hard drives have to worry about as all hard drives for the A1200 do this automatically.

In an extreme case the hard disk can be ruined and will need replacement. They aren't practical to repair and, when something mechanical starts to go wrong, it isn't going to fix itself.

If the hard disk does *crash* you will normally be informed of the glum news by repeated disk error messages and an inability to access certain areas of data. What has happened is the data used to store some of your files has been partially destroyed. Depending on where the crash occurs this may be an annoying niggle or a total catastrophe. In the case of the former it may be quite possible to save a lot of data; in the latter you may have to completely reformat your hard disk.

Backing Up

If you thought that the dangers of disk damage were bad enough on a floppy disk just wait until you get a hard drive. You have vast amounts of storage space which is great in normal circumstances, less so when something goes wrong. Suffering a hard disk crash and watching as your work disappears is heartbreaking. If something does go wrong then you will want to have a copy of as much as possible of what has been lost.

The most obvious way of doing this is to copy the entire hard disk onto a series of floppy disks at regular intervals. You can do this but it will soon become laborious. If you have files larger than the 878K that fits onto a floppy disk then quite simply you won't be able to do it.

Fortunately there are several programs available which will do the job for you and can also keep track of which of your files actually need backing up.

A backup program copies the partition or even part of it onto a series of floppy disks. These can then be kept somewhere safe. Then, after a reasonable interval when you wish to update your backup, you can use the same disks and the program will only add that data which has been changed from the time of the previous backup. So, although backing up for the first time is relatively slow, on any subsequent occasions it can be quite rapid. Restoring a file from its backup is just a matter of selecting the appropriate option from the program and then feeding it disks as it demands.

There are several backup systems available but they all do much the same job. Some of them have the option of incorporating a file compression routine into the process. The advantage of this is that your data can be squeezed onto fewer disks. The disadvantage is that it takes longer because the A1200 has to take time actually doing the compression and decompression. Swings and roundabouts.

One further subtlety. Many hard drive users will backup one partition onto another. The theory here is that it is unlikely for both partitions to be damaged at the same time and the process is much faster. However doing it this way means taking up space on the hard drive that you will want to use for better purposes. It is up to you but you may want to consider keeping a backup of just your most recent work on a separate partition to save time.

Other Possibilities

So far this chapter has been mainly concerned with the addition of an internal IDE hard drive to your A1200. There are, however, other possibilities. You should also read the "Improve Your Memory" chapter on adding extra RAM to the machine and perhaps consider the cheaper option of adding an extra floppy disk instead. These processes offer different advantages to the hard drive but are similar in that they offer speed increases in the overall computing process, albeit in very different ways.

Another option which may become more popular is the use of removable hard disks. These don't fit internally for obvious reasons! The set-up is very similar to fitting an additional floppy drive except that the disks which fit in this drive are typically of 40Mb each and have all the usual hard disk advantages of ultra-rapid speed. The drive itself is the expensive part with additional hard disks being relatively cheap. This sort of set-up is particularly useful if you are in the habit of either a) working on completely unrelated projects which rule out the possibility of having to keep swapping between hard disks or b) exchanging large files with another computer similarly equipped.

Another option is that of optical disks. These drives use a different technology to read and write to CD style disks. In behaviour they are similar to removable hard drives, are considerably slower in their access times but have far larger capacity.

There are other options available in the world of hard drives: the chapter *Improve Your Memory* discusses the advantage of fitting a hard drive via the PCMCIA port whilst one can also be fitted to the parallel port. This second option means that the hard drive has slow access speeds and cannot be used for booting from. However, it may be useful as a means of having a data back-up.

Hard Disk Set-ups

The concept of customising the A1200 Workbench should by now be very familiar. With a hard disk all the old options are still there only more so. Booting off a floppy disk meant having everything you needed squeezed onto the one disk. Space on a hard drive isn't limitless but it's considerably more than on a floppy disk. That means that any specifications you want to make to Workbench and any programs you want included in the startup process are easily executed. You can incorporate an attractive screen image as the backdrop to the Workbench window and replace the feeble Amiga "beep" with your own more theatrical sound effects without worrying about disk space. Don't get too carried away though, as all these refinements do make demands on the machine RAM.

Problem Solving

Some IDE drives that can be fitted inside an A1200 aren't quite up to the task. The problem is that they were designed to fit in portable PCs and can't physically cope with the speed with which the A1200 throws data at them. Should this happen then programs that you try to run from the hard drive – particularly ones which involve the moving around of large files – may tend to crash. In most cases it's not an insoluble problem and can be solved by altering the "MaxTransfer" rate within the HDToolBox or similar application. Try setting it to 0x20000. If this doesn't solve your problems then the difficulty may lie within the software itself. Some software isn't designed to run from a hard drive but in most cases there will be a utility available from its authors which will install it for you. In the worst cases you may have to go back to running from a floppy. This is increasingly rare, however, and shouldn't happen with commercial software.

Insider Guide #20: The Workbench partition.

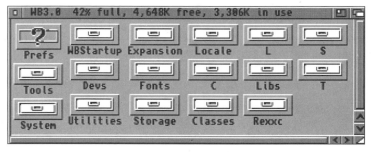

The Workbench partition of the hard disk should appear as shown at the top whilst beneath it is the same window using the "Show >> All Files" options. This partition should contain all that normally appears on the Workbench, Extras, Storage, Fonts and Locale disks.

Make sure that this partition is comfortably larger than those disks – say 6Mb in total so that room is made available for extra fonts and utilities that may be useful. With more space to play around with on the boot disk, extra utilities can be placed in the WBStartup directory.

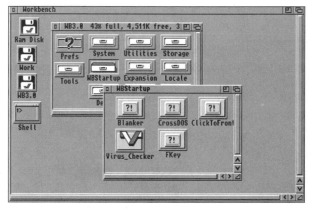

Up and Running

Now that the hard drive is installed and working smoothly, some of the instructions in this book will have to be altered to make sense. The Workbench and Extras disk have effectively merged to become one big directory and the Storage, Locale and Fonts disks have become subdirectories within this. So, when you read "Insert the Storage disk" the instruction becomes "Open the Storage directory" instead. You'll find that it is much faster.

Insider Guide #21: Backup with ABackup.

This utility is simplicity itself. Double-click on the icon to launch it and select "Backup an AmigaDOS Partition" from the menu.

Select the disk, partition or directory you wish to back up using the file display. You can toggle between the current directory and the Workbench using the righthand mouse button outside this viewer.

Press OK to start the process.

From the next screen select the files you wish to save and then click on "Start". You are then asked to choose which disk drive you wish to save to. Feed the disk drive with blank disks as you are prompted until completion.

Restoring a file follows a similar procedure but starting with the "Restore a partition" option.

17 Improve Your Memory

Multitasking isn't multitasking unless you've got room for a multitiude of tasks. An extra dose of RAM is called for...

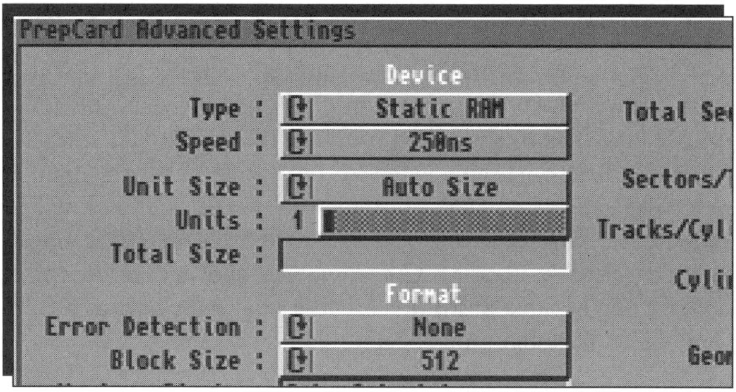
PrepCard Advanced Settings
Device
Type : Static RAM
Speed : 250ns
Unit Size : Auto Size
Units : 1
Total Size :
Format
Error Detection : None
Block Size : 512
Total Se
Sectors/
Tracks/Cyl
Cyli
Geo

The A1200 has been touted as the ultimate graphics machine. With its new AGA graphics chips it offers abilities which were previously unheard of on a home computer.

One of the drawbacks of graphics processing, however, is that graphics files tend to be enormous. It may well be feasible to squeeze the entire works of Shakespeare onto a hard disk but the I-Spy Book of Birds will probably take up far more space. As a means of efficiently storing pictorial information, printed matter still takes some beating.

The large size of graphics files is one reason behind the decision to fit the A1200 with 2Mb of RAM as standard. It's a quantity that only a few years ago would have been thought excessive. That's progress.

What makes graphics files so large is not just their physical dimensions of width by height but also the number of colours they incorporate. If you are regularly juggling with large files of this nature – perhaps in a DTP package – it won't be long before that 2Mb seems restrictive.

How to Fit Them

Most RAM expansion cards are *trap-door* expansions. The trap-door is found underneath the A1200. To fit one of these expansions first switch the A1200 off and disconnect it from everything. Open the trap-door and look inside the machine at the opposite end of the trap-door to the securing catch. You should be able to see two flat, broad plates protruding. The expansion card slots onto these plates. The operation is by no means difficult it's just that it can appear daunting when the expansion card appears much bigger than the trap-door it has to squeeze through. With the card fitted the increase in RAM should be acknowledged on the Workbench menu bar. When buying expansion RAM you may want to consider adding a maths co-processor. Most expansion RAM cards have space to fit one of these bolt-on go-faster goodies. Other features and details to look out for when buying expansion RAM is a battery-backed clock, a SCSI interface and the card's maximum capacity.

With a battery-backed clock fitted the Clock and Time utilities come into their own. A SCSI interface can be used to add on additional hard drives or perhaps a tape streamer. It's not going to be first choice for most people but probably an essential for *power users*. The card's maximum capacity has to be considered carefully before purchase. Try and consider possible future requirements and the maximum RAM you might ever need and make sure that the expansion you buy can be upgraded to this figure.

PCMCIA

PCMCIA, what is it? Well, the abbreviation stands for the surprisingly non-technical Personal Computer Memory Card International Association. And that's all it is – an industry standard just like any of the others you might have met such as SCSI or MIDI.

What it means in practice is that the makers of the cards and of those machines which would like to use them have got together to make sure that the bits and pieces are compatible across the whole spectrum of machines. Commodore have adhered to this standard by equipping the Amiga A1200 with a a slot on the lefthand side of the keyboard which can accept PCMCIA cards. If you look to the left of your machine you will see that, sure enough, there is a 68-pin slot, the PCMCIA slot.

Like the other ports on the machine this slot can potentially be used to add on all sorts of goodies: modems, hard drives etc. Anything, in fact which has been designed and built to accept the PCMCIA standard. So what is there to get excited about? The PCMCIA standard just so happens to be the standard employed by *smart cards*. If you haven't heard of them yet, smart cards are those gadgets which we keep being told are set to replace credit cards, passports, keys and goodness knows what else all on one electronic plastic card. Similar in dimensions to a credit card, though much thicker, smart cards are capable of storing several megabytes of information – enough for most day to day needs.

The idea is that users will just plug their cards into the supermarket cash till or wherever for direct transferal of funds. Attached to the electronics of the user's car, the same card will be able to render the vehicle inoperable simply by its absence. Say goodbye to joy-riders. And I'm sure there are endless other uses that you can think of which they might conceivably be put to.

Memory Cards

As computer users our interest in PCMCIA technology lies with the "memory" part of the PCMCIA acronym. At its simplest it means that a card can be plugged into the side of the Amiga and – hey presto! – an instant memory upgrade. Already there are several makes of memory card which can be used in this manner. To fit one couldn't be simpler. Switch off your Amiga and gently slide the card face up into the socket. Whatever you do, don't try and fit one – or any other hardware upgrade for that matter – whilst the machine is switched on. Don't push the card in too hard either. The socket will most probably be reasonably firm, particularly when first used but, when the card won't go any further, stop pushing. There's no tell-tale click to tell you that it's in all the way. If it's in no danger of falling out then it's in far enough. Now switch the machine back on. If the card is a 2Mb card then the Workbench bar legend should read something along the lines of: "Amiga Workbench 1,984,520 graphics mem, 1,946,6472 other mem." Not to worry if the figures on your machine don't quite match mine.

The "other mem" is that additional memory supplied by the PCMCIA card.

As a means of boosting the memory size of your Amiga it really takes some beating. To fit an ordinary upgrade sometimes requires taking the machine to pieces. If your dealer does it for you then it takes time and money (time is money, don't forget) and a trip to the dealership itself. Do the job yourself and you invalidate the machine's warranty by breaking those stickers where the two parts join together. But fitting a PCMCIA card takes seconds and does not invalidate the warranty. For this very reason PCMCIA cards are liable to catch on.

The Down Side

There are, however, several serious drawbacks that need to be voiced. Use the PCMCIA slot for a memory expansion and you won't be able to use it for anything else. This may or may not be a problem and all depends on what you envisage using your machine for. Secondly you may not like the idea of a vital component sticking out of the side of your computer in what appears to be such a vulnerable position. I can picture the situation now... It's late in the evening, you've been sat facing the machine for so long you're going bleary-eyed, you lean forward to stare at the screen more closely, cupping your chin in your hands and resting your elbows on what you thought was going to be the table. Crunch. Ooops, there goes several hours work and one trashed smart card. Does this sound as though it could be you?

PCMCIA cards are a more expensive means of upgrading memory, for the time being, though this may change significantly if and when they become mass produced. The final and most important consideration is that of speed. The A1200 is a state of the art home computer fitted with a 32-bit processor which means it's fast. PCMCIA cards, however, are not. They rely on 16-bit design and that means they will slow your machine down. Not vitally important if you're using it for wordprocessing but a killer if you're into ray tracing.

Other Uses

Plug-in memory is only one part of the story. A PCMCIA card of this fashion is called a Static RAM or SRAM card. "Static" meaning stationary because you can't move it

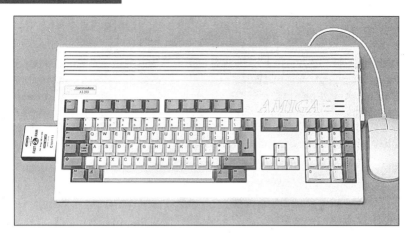

Above: A plug-in memory card is quick and easy to install but you may decide that the PCMCIA slot is better used for other expansions such as a hard drive.

Below: Many, more conventional, RAM expansions can be fitted via the trap door beneath the A1200. This may require a little manouevring as the expansion cards can be bigger than the hole itself. Make sure the machine is switched off first.

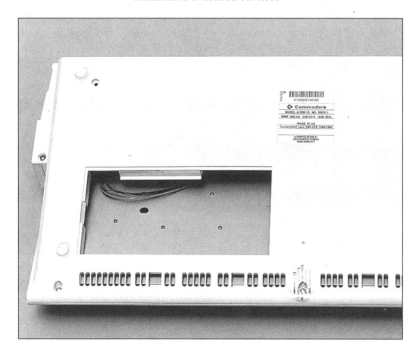

around, it just sits there like any other part of memory. Switch the machine off and any data it contains is lost for good.

But the whole point of smart card technology is that you can plug one into a terminal, perform some transaction which maybe updates information stored on card, and take it away for use another time, another place. Such cards are called Dynamic RAM or DRAM cards. As yet they are not available for the A1200 but Commodore anticipate that they will arrive at some unspecified date in the future.

Just a Wee Dram

The main difference between SRAM and DRAM cards is that the DRAM cards are battery backed. This means that any information stored on them is retained as long as the battery is alive; however long that might be. Their use is inherently different from SRAM cards in that they can be plugged into and pulled out of the machine when it is switched on with no risk of damage to card, machine or data. Most importantly – and this is the clever bit – DRAM cards can be configured to act either as memory, just like their humble SRAM cousins, or they can be configured to behave just like an extra drive. Used as an extra drive, you could save files to a DRAM card or even use it to boot up your machine from, leaving the floppy drive free for other use. Booting up from a DRAM card is going to be so much faster than the endless grinding of the floppy disk drive alternative.

There is a drawback at the moment and it's quite a major one at that. Using a DRAM card as a glorified floppy disk is akin to using a sledgehamer to crack a nut. A few megabytes of DRAM and you can kiss goodbye to a hundred quid. Floppy disks, by comparison, are given away free with packets of cornflakes... almost.

But, as with all new technologies, the situation can change very quickly. Expect prices to tumble over the next few years and maybe this won't appear such a white elephant after all.

There are other forms of PCMCIA cards in the offing – particularly EEPROM (Electrical Erasable One-time Programmable Read Only Memory) cards. All that this mouthful means is that information can be recorded onto one of these cards once and only once. Not a whole lot of use to the end user but just the sort of thing manufacturers will be looking for to put their games and other programs onto. The advantages will not just be the speed of access – which can be a pain with games, particularly those that need more than one disk – but also the ability to squeeze more information onto one card than onto one disk will surely make them popular. Whether it makes an impact on the levels of software piracy remains to be seen.

PrepCard

To set up a DRAM card for use will require the use of the PrepCard utility which is to be found on the A1200 Extras Disk in the "Tools" directory. Double-clicking on the PrepCard icon brings up a window listing information about whatever device is in the PCMCIA slot. Simply clicking the "Prepare as DISK" button will do just that: formatting the card as though it were a floppy disk in its drive.

The card can then be used as any other disk. The PCMCIA slot is accorded the device name of CC0: and the card is by default called "Empty". As with formatting a floppy disk the program pops up a warning before it tries to configure the card stating that this action will erase any information stored on the card. And, again like floppy disks, DRAM cards will be equipped with physical write-protection tabs on their sides to prevent accidental destruction of vital files.

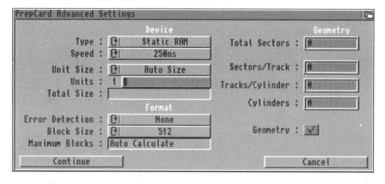

Figure 17.1. The Prepcard Window.

A DRAM card will also be configurable as Static RAM simply by clicking the "Prepare as System RAM" button. The machine won't immediately recognise its existence but, on rebooting, the extra memory will be acknowledged on the icon bar at the top of the Workbench screen. Let me give just one final note of caution. If you do this then the rules of SRAM cards apply once again. Try and remove a DRAM card configured as SRAM and the machine will crash destroying all that work that you forgot to save.

A Hard Choice

The PCMCIA slot can be used to plug in a suitably manufactured hard drive. This has several advantages over an internal expansion:

1. You can do it yourself without invalidating your warranty – it just plugs in.

2. Larger disks can be used. Typically this will mean the 3.5 inch IDE drives rather than the 2.5 inch IDE drives that have to be fitted internally. The larger drives are cheaper on a cost per RAM basis.

3. The PCMCIA interface allows for rapid transfer of data. Hard drives fitted in this way are as quick as you can get.

4. A hard drive can be fitted via the PCMCIA slot in addition to any other hard drive already fitted.

18

Put the A1200 at the heart of your home video editing suite...

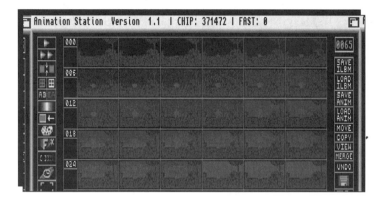

*T*he one, single feature above all others which originally made the Amiga so popular as a home computer was its ability to handle graphics. Its colourful displays and the ease with which images could be manipulated and moved around the screen made it the natural choice for anyone wanting to write games. The manufacturers took one look at it and knew there and then that it was the machine to follow.

And in terms of games playing the Amiga is still an excellent choice. The availability of keyboard, mouse and joystick means that, whatever the game, the A1200 is an ideal machine. But there is much more to graphics than pretty games no matter how good they may be. Amiga owners have quickly grasped the potential that the machine has for creating and manipulating their own images.

Graphic Images

In addition to software which lets you use the mouse as a paintbrush and the screen as your easel there are packages which generate imaginary landscapes from user-defined variables. These fractal generators employ mathematics from the same source as Mandelbrot sets – based on the in-vogue chaos theory.

Raytracing is a slow but popular method of producing photo-realistic scenes. These are generated by defining all the objects being viewed in geometric terms and then calculating how the ambient light, and its reflections, will make each appear. The end results of these scenes look real – too real, somehow – but takes hours to process.

Morphing is the latest fad in animation. It involves taking two screen images and laboriously mapping features from one onto the other. The software then processes the changeover from one image to the other. Used well these can make one face slowly distort until it becomes another. Used poorly and the picture of a chair will unconvincingly become one of a spaceship.

Animation

Having created a series of attractive pictures or a set of animations there remains the problem of how to display them. Wouldn't it be ideal to be able to record these images – static or moving – onto the video recorder (VCR) and play them back at leisure without all the trouble of loading from sets of disks and waiting for software to process files? Of course it would, and the A1200 can do just that for you, although you will need one or two extra pieces of hardware.

Depending on your ambition and – let's be honest – the size of your wallet, the A1200 can be linked to all manner of video gadgetry. At the most basic level you will want to be able to record images from the computer screen directly onto a video recorder. All you require for this, in principle, is an encoder which will convert the computer's screen information into one which the VCR can understand. In the UK this format is called PAL and in the USA it is called NTSC. So, depending on where you are, you'll need either a PAL encoder or an NTSC encoder. This device usually plugs into the back of the A1200 via the RGB monitor port

With one fitted the VCR will record, in real time, the events happening on the Amiga's screen. You might use it to keep a record of how a particular game was played, for example, or to store a library of your computer artwork.

From Television

To perform the process in reverse calls for the services of a video digitiser. With this piece of hardware connected to your A1200 you can grab images directly from video or television. This opens up a whole new area of computer potential. Once you can take images from a TV source, they can be manipulated with the A1200 and then re-recorded in their altered state. Thus the A1200 can be used as an integral part of a video editing suite.

To digitise a picture takes a finite time so if you are trying to grab from live TV the first problem you will encounter is trying to find a still screen. The whole purpose of television is, of course, to transmit moving images but, unfortunately the more they move the harder they are to digitise. It's like trying to take a photograph with a slow shutter speed, if your subject doesn't keep still you end up with blurred photos. You can always use a VCR and then digitise from a freezed frame but you do need to have a VCR with a high quality, flicker-free, pause facility.

So, in theory you could grab a screen from a video source, digitise it into a format the A1200 is happy with and having manipulated the image in some way – for example in DPaintIV – rerecord it back to video. More probably the two processes will be used independently. The encoder will be used to make a record of what has been produced on the A1200 and the digitiser used as a good source of images for use in paint packages, desktop publishing programs and the like.

Digitising

There are a couple of points to bear in mind, however. The first is that the image a digitiser produces on the computer screen is of a different quality to that on the VCR. It will have that "digitised" look which means that the image will be blockier, ie looking more like it is made up from small coloured blocks. The second difficulty is that a certain degree of colour may be lost.

The A1200 is equipped with many different screen modes, each of which is capable of displaying a given number of colours. At its most primitive this can be just two colours – black and white with not even a trace of grey. If this mode is used then each screen pixel, as it is digitised, is assessed to see whether it is going to be represented by either a black or a white pixel on the computer screen.

You can make the decision about what the A1200 uses as its threshold for this process but the end result will still be a black and white picture, without greys. Fine, if you're looking for some special effect, a silhouetted image perhaps, but not a lot of use otherwise.

Clearly there's no need to limit ourselves to two-colour images and with the higher resolution colour screen modes the computer image can appear every bit as colourful as the original providing the digitiser is up to the task. The pay-off is the time that this all takes; the more complex the image the longer the wait. And the longer the wait the larger the resulting file. A graphics file can soon become too big to store on floppy disk and, if this is your objective, some sort of compromise will have to be reached.

Camcorders

Digitising need not be restricted to getting images from a VCR – the camcorder is an equally valid source. The advantage of being able to use a camcorder in this way is not just that you can record images from real-life. You also effectively have a second video player and are thus well on the way to building up a complete home video editing suite.

The A1200 can combine the signal from a VCR with another it has generated internally and record them on a second VCR. Not only that but it can also make sure that the two signals are synchronised to the user's specifications. To do this requires a genlock. This black box device monitors the signal arriving from the one video source and then watches out for the right times to add its own contribution.

Typically this can be used for adding titles to home video footage but needn't stop there. In the same way that the lettering of a title masks part of the image on-screen so different shapes can be used to create other special effects or to chop off part of the original image. What the genlock does is remove one of the colours from the computer screen and replace it with the VCR image.

Let's say, for the sake of argument, that you've just got back from a rather nice holiday in Bali (dream on). You have plenty of video footage but you need to add a few titles. Using one of the software packages available you write the word "BALI" as red lettering on a black background and then set up the genlock to replace the black during the introduction to your video. If the lettering for your title is suitably big and chunky you might even try it the other way round. Select a font which produces overlapping block capitals big enough to fill the screen and this time set the genlock to replace the red of the lettering rather than the black of the background. Experiment with it and see what happens.

Masking off parts of the screen in this way can be used to create all sorts of interesting effects. James Bond movies traditionally start with that rather naff piece of film where he's tracked through a gunsight, something which you might want to improve on yourself. The screen could similarly be shaped to suggest the "looking through binoculars" effect or narrowed to look like a wide-screen film format. A genlock with appropriate software may also be used to provide fade outs. With any of these tricks though they must be used sparingly or they lose their impact.

As you become more proficient at video techniques you will want to expand the capabilities of your set-up. What about the computer taking total control of the video player and video recorder and combining video images and graphics at its own pace? Yet again the A1200 is up to the challenge and this is the stage where we leave the realm of home enthusiast and enter the world of professional video editing because the A1200 can be used to take complete control of both sound and visual output. There is no limit to what can be achieved.

Producing an animation on computer usually requires some form of compromise. At the cinema the effect of animation is produced by showing a series of static images, all subtly different from the previous one, and displaying them quickly enough so that the brain is fooled into thinking it is seeing a smoothly moving image. This is no different from those animated stick figure drawings you used to produce in the margins of books at school (what do you mean, you still do?). The Amiga A1200 produces its animations in exactly the same way.

The difficulty is that it takes a finite time for a computer to display an image on screen – this is called the screen refresh rate, the time taken to completely redraw the screen image. As you will have experienced from using paint packages such as DPaint or by viewing files in MultiView the process of drawing a picture on screen can be quite slow. The more complex the image and the more colours involved then the slower it becomes. If this has to happen every time a frame advances then the so-called animation will just become a series of jerky images. Not only that but the computer has to store all these images in its memory in advance of showing them. With anything above the simplest animation the normal supply of memory quickly becomes exhausted.

Look Out, Disney!

Fortunately those folk who program the A1200 are a resourceful bunch and all manner of cheats and tricks have been dreamed up to help find a way round these problems.

In most animations the image on screen is virtually unchanged from one frame to the next. Delta animation is a technique whereby the initial frame is recorded but the only part of the second frame that is stored are those places where it differs from the first frame. Each subsequent frame is simply stored as a record of how it differs from the preceding one. With less memory clogged with images, animations can be longer. If the animated parts are reduced in size then the difference between frames will be reduced further – a large object moving around will demand more redrawing than a smaller one. Why is this sort of animation called *delta*? Well, in Mathematics, the greek letter Delta is used to denote the amount by which a variable changes given a certain set of circumstances; Delta – a measure of change.

Other tricks include reducing the size of the screen that the animation uses, repeating parts of the animation (looping) and limiting the number of colours used in the animation. But with all that done it is still difficult to produce a decent cartoon of more than a few seconds without running out of memory. Your best bet in these circumstances is to save your animation to video tape frame by frame. This way you need no longer worry about screen refresh rates, restricting yourself to limited-colour productions or using small cartoon characters – if you have the patience you can do exactly what you like.

This sort of set-up will give you complete control over the video image that you produce and the quality of end product will be directly proportional to the amount of effort that you are prepared to put in in the first place.

Sounds Good

Finally, having made the perfect film, you will want to add a soundtrack. Again this can be one which you have produced on the Amiga. The subject of sound production is dealt with in the "Sounds Good" chapter but it is enough to know at this stage that the finished product can be synchronised with the final video image using combined digitising/sound sampling hardware. At the professional level something called SMPTE code brings together soundtrack and video frames into a seamless whole. Professional prices will buy you this ability!

Graphics Cards

A graphics card is a piece of hardware that can be plugged into your Amiga. It takes over the displaying of images on screen and its primary effect is to offer more colour – much more colour. With top-end 24-bit graphics cards you should be able to display all the colours on screen that you will ever need.

It is important to be aware that not all software will be able to exploit the potential of a graphics card unless it has been specifically written to do just that. Fortunately the makers of graphics cards also provide software modules, often available as part of the overall package. But this may mean that you won't be able to use, say, your favourite paint package or animation program with a particular card – a point to bear in mind before purchase.

The other thing to remember is that it is no good having enormous graphics capabilities without a suitable monitor to display it all on. The minimum requirement is one of Commodore's dual-sync monitors.

In theory everything that you can do on the *ordinary* A1200 you should also be able to do on one fitted with a graphics card. This includes the whole gamut of video manipulations. If you are seriously considering using your A1200 at the heart of a video editing suite using 24-bit colour images then you will need a specifically designed graphics card, the best known of which is the *Video Toaster*. At several times the price of the A1200 itself a video toaster is a combined graphics card and video editing suite. You can use one to edit videos in real-time displaying all the colours; you can flip images, perform wipes, fades and dissolves. In fact a Video Toaster can do pretty well everything except make toast.

Insider Guide #22: Video hardware combinations

1. *The most basic set-up uses a PAL encoder to record computer images onto a VCR.*

2. *Reversing the process calls for a video digitiser.*

3. *A genlock co-ordinates signals between two video devices.*

4. *Go wild. The A1200 can be at the heart of a video editing suite.*

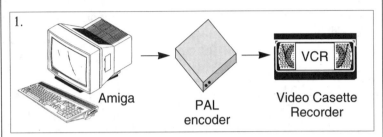

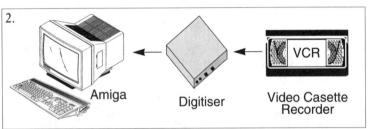

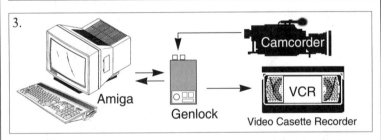

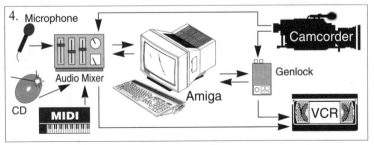

19

Computer music isn't just techno. The choice of style is all yours – roll over, Beethoven!

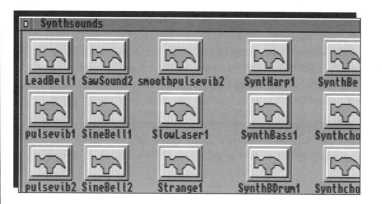

*C*omputer music is nothing new. Tubular Bells was a big hit in the early 70s for Mike Oldfield while Jean Michel Jarre has been churning out albums for more years than he or anyone else cares to mention. The advent of house music has made the computer an accepted part of the paraphernalia of the modern musician. All of which can give a distorted perception about what can be achieved on computer. You might take one look at the artistes' names above, decide that their style of music isn't to your liking, and dismiss the whole phenomenon. Which would be a shame because the A1200 can be used to write and play music of pretty well any variety you care to mention. Violin quartets? No problem.

In recent years the CD has replaced the vinyl disc as the foremost medium for storing music. The important part of this technology for computer musicians is that the music is stored in a digital format. This means that everything you hear is stored as a series of digital pulses, exactly the same sort of data that is the lifeblood of computing.

Sampling

Sampling is the means by which *live* sound can be captured for use on the A1200. Obviously some hardware is called for and, in this case, it's a small device – called a sampler – which plugs into the parallel port at the back of the A1200. Cables can then connect the sampler with a hi-fi, personal stereo or microphone.

The sampling process is normally controlled from the computer keyboard and all it does is make a digital recording of whatever sound is being produced. This is then represented on the screen as a waveform. You will probably need to repeat this process several times to ensure that the wave almost but not quite reaches the maximum recording level. Above this limit and the loudest parts are lost ("clipping") making the end result sound fuzzy. Too far beneath this limit and the sound feels muted and clarity is lost.

With the perfect sample now recorded, the software should let you edit this to your satisfaction. Most packages will let you cut out any unwanted parts so that only the part of the note you actually want remains.

Let's say, for the sake of argument, that you wanted to sample a cymbal crash from a piece of music on CD. With the CD player connected to the sampler, press the CD's "Play" button and then, from the A1200 keyboard, press "Record" and then "Stop" either side of that note. The waveform shown is a picture of that sound and you can experiment with cutting off various bits of the sound until you are left with just the sound that you want.

You can play this note over and over again adjusting the cut-off points by fractional amounts until you have it to perfection. The sound can now be saved in the IFF (Interchange File Format) format which other programs on your A1200, and elsewhere, will recognise.

Sampling well is something of an art, particularly if you are using a microphone to record live sounds when you want to sample a particular sound but without any of the background noise. Experimentation is the key and you will quickly find that where you position the microphone and the sampling rate both have a major impact.

Many computer musicians, though, are quite happy to let others get on with the sampling, leaving themselves to slave away building these samples into meaningful tunes. The public domain is thick with IFF sound files that have been sampled from every conceivable source.

Any musical instrument that you care to mention is there along with snatches of movie soundtracks, special effects and original synthesised sounds. Admittedly they are of variable quality but they do tend to be very cheap. The only real drawback with samples like these is their size. A short note on a recorder produces a tiny file but the more complex, and longer, a sound is the larger the file size. Too may large files and you will soon find yourself running out of memory space.

Trackers

Having amassed a selection of sounds that you want to incorporate into your song the next step is to find a means of playing them. IFF sound files can be played via MultiView should you so wish but that's all you can do with it, they can't be manipulated in any constructive way. What is really called for is a piece of software called a "Tracker".

The most famous of these on the Amiga is Teijo Kinunnen's OctaMED. It is famous not just because it is so good but also because it is available in the public domain. If you are interested in finding out about your A1200's sound capabilities without laying out exorbitant amounts of cash then there's no better place to start. Whichever tracker you choose, though, the principle behind them is pretty much the same.

Writing Music

Taking one instrument at a time a tracker lets you decide when each note is to be sounded. Time itself is divided up into a series of steps and there can be as many steps as you want and as close together or as far apart as you chose. Step Zero is the first note of the tune, song or track – call it what you will – with Step One being the next available occasion to make a noise. In principle the tracker is a series of instructions like:

Step One: Hit the bass drum, play penny whistle (note A) and crash the cymbal

Step Two: Hit the snare drum and play the penny whistle (note C#)

Step Three: Sound the gong

Step Four: Penny whistle (note D)

              Repeat Steps One to Four three times then

Step Five   Sound the fire alarm

Step Six   ... and so on

The above would sound awful but you get the idea. To construct a very simple song you might choose to have a bass drum sound on Steps 0, 4, 8, 12, 16 etc and a snare drum to sound on steps 2, 6, 10, 14, 18 and so on. The net effect would be a very straighforward thump-crash thump-crash beat. Next you can add a few musical instruments. Each instrument should be assigned a separate track and the tracker simply keeps details of when which notes on which instruments are to be played, how long they are to be played for, how loudly (relative to each other) and at what frequency (or pitch) they are to be played.

As with any other computer software there is the facility to let the computer take the monotony out of repetitive tasks. You might have one drum rhythm for the verse and one for the chorus. Simply label these as A and B and the Tracker will be able to play sequences like AABAABBA or ABABABBA as you dictate. Whole blocks can be copied quickly letting you get on with the creative side of things. If the melody is being played by one instrument and you decide you want to change it to a different one then that's no problem either. The Tracker lets you play back all or just sections of the track as you choose. It is very easy to build up repetitive loops of music which is why this approach has been so popular in writing dance music but there's no reason why it needs to be limited to just this.

Progressing

If you think of the Tracker as being a control panel to a library of sounds then you have a fair idea of how it works. However, the A1200 isn't limited to just using the sounds it has stored in memory.

Suitably equipped the A1200 can be connected to external sound sources, such as an electronic keyboard, a drum machine or synthesiser and can be used to control what they play. The means by which this is done is via the MIDI system.

MIDI simply stands for Musical Instrument Digital Interface and it is another industry standard like PCMCIA or SCSI. The theory is that anything fitted with a MIDI port can be attached to anything else with a MIDI port and that the two can *talk*. In our example this would mean that the A1200 could direct a synthesiser to play certain notes at

Insider Guide #23: Getting started with OctaMED.

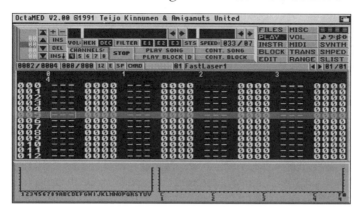

OctaMED is a hugely powerful, and therefore complex, piece of software. It will take hours of use to fully master all its features.

The opening screen has various panels to click on in the top right-hand corner. Click on "Files" and the options presented include the ability to load files – pre-written songs or sound samples – and to save your own work. The "Play" option lets you hear what you have selected. Samples can be played using the A1200 keyboard as a piano keyboard:

```
23      567     90                      =\
        Q W E R T Y U I O P
S D     G H J                   L ;
        Z X C V B N M , . /
```

One octave is above the other. The "Edit" and "Block" options are where the construction of a song takes place. Further options allow the output to be displayed in a variety of manners to suit your own preferences.

certain times while instructing a drum machine to provide the accompanying beat and filling in with some sampled sounds of its own.

To do this sort of impressive feat requires not just the external instruments (which must be of the MIDI variety) but also a MIDI interface for the A1200 and the appropriate software which is called a Sequencer. This is where music starts to become expensive on the Amiga but is also where the sound quality enters the professional category. Not only do sequencers offer you control over external instruments but you can also play a tune on one of these instruments – ie play a tune on a keyboard – and record this on the computer. The sequencer will then adjust its timing to fit that of the song you are writing.

Singing

To raise the pitch of a note is just a simple matter of increasing its frequency. Sample a Middle C from a piano and double its frequency and it will sound one octave higher. Unfortunately it will no longer sound much like the equivalent note on the piano. A piano has many overtones that all contribute to its rich and distinctive sound. Many samplers make allowances for this and let the user sample at several different frequencies and then use all this information to calculate the intervening notes that approximate to the real sound.

The most complex note though has to be the human voice. It wouldn't be so bad if all we ever sang were plain notes – lah lah lah lah laaah – but these songwriting chappies always seem to insist on using words. If you are using your A1200 for serious songwriting like this then you are better off adding the vocal track last, at the tape stage.

Guitars are similarly difficult to mimic, particulary if they are used with effects pedals, as they can produce a very broad variety of sounds. *Multi-timbral* as the musicians would say.

The opposite is true for drums which traditionally have little variation in sound. Using a tracker as a drum machine is simplicity itself. However, as it lets you alter the pitch of the drums, just like any other instrument, there is no reason why you shouldn't do so. It may sound dreadful, it may sound great but until you experiment with it there's no way of finding out.

File Formats

Most samplers produce data in a *raw* format which they can understand but is of little use to anything else. As the ability to exchange files between programs is fundamental to music-making on computer a standard format is used. This is normally the IFF 8SVX format – the "8" refers to 8-bit which is sample resolution. As 16-bit sampling becomes more commonplace another file type is needed – the AudioIFF format as it is called. It may not be important to know the technical details of how these files are read and so on, only that they do differ and that you must have suitable software should you wish to use them.

20

Take a break from the more serious side of computing and check out some of the entertainment...

CARRIES FOUR FULLY EQUIPPED PLATOONS INTO BATTLE.
TYPE : B-29 BATTLE CRUISER

*O*k, so this is supposed to be a serious book. It is also intended to be a guide to getting more out of your Amiga A1200 and that has to include playing games. Yes, the A1200 can do all the serious stuff like wordprocessing, spreadsheeting, databasing (if such a word exists) and programming. It can also perform the more glamorous options such as writing and playing music, video editing and image creation. But when it comes to games-playing the A1200 is *the* home computer and if you're not using it as such then you're missing out.

All Work, No Play

Don't be fooled into thinking that games are just for the kids and require lightning fast reflexes and unbelievable dexterity with a joystick. Such games exist – and can be great fun – but whatever your level of enjoyment there's going to be a welter of games to suit. As the A1200 offers you the choice of keyboard, mouse or joystick input or a combination of them it is considerably more flexible than its console alternatives.

I've tried to describe the main categories of games but as designers get more and more sophisticated in their approach, pigeon-holing their products becomes more and more difficult. The best games often incorporate features of many, if not all, of the types below.

Joystick Wagglers

Most of these challenge the user's hand-eye coordination by repeating the same demands but at subtly increased levels of difficulty each time around. As you progress onto harder levels of the game you will often find that your range of choices expands. Whilst this increases your ability to tackle whatever is thrown against you, it does give you more to think about...

Shoot-em-ups

As the description suggests the main aim in this type of game is to shoot at anything that moves and often quite a lot that doesn't. Typically you control a space ship which is armed with one or more offensive weapons. Traditionally this moves from left to right – or more accurately, the background moves from right to left – and can be controlled either from the computer keyboard or by a joystick. The objective is normally to score as many points as possible by shooting down ever-increasing numbers of alien craft. A variety of bonuses are often available allowing you to increase your firepower at vital moments.

Platform Games

In these you control some form of character who walks back and forth along various levels (or platforms), hopping over obstacles, blasting aliens, collecting items and jumping between different levels. There is usually a specific objective in the game and a certain element of puzzle-solving to be done on the way. For example you might have to pick up a key to unlock a door, or some money to purchase another item. One common complication is that you are limited to carrying a set number of items around with you and so have to calculate what you will need and when you will need them. All this whilst dodging enemies and occasionally fighting the clock makes for cerebral overload.

Beat-em-ups

You are the Karate Ninja Death Kid or some equally implausible hero. Your quest is to beat up a large percentage of the world's population and stamp out Evil while wearing just a blood-stained headband and a leather thong, or something along those lines. Best when played with a joystick this differs from platform games in the manoeuvrability of the leading character. Moving the joystick in the right direction at the right time makes the on-screen character perform all manner of chops, kicks, leaps and punches. Master this part of the game and you're well on your way to success.

Sports Simulations

Football, Ice-Hockey, Snooker, Car Racing, Stoat Wrestling, you name it – if it's a recognised sport then someone somewhere has written a simulation for it. In the example of the football games that have proliferated you are in charge of the entire team but only actually control one individual on the field at any one time – usually the one nearest the ball – with the A1200 doing the rest. The options in this sort of game are endless – you can decide on the formation you're team will play in, make substitutions, deliberately foul opponents and so on while the better games will also include doubtful refereeing decisions. It's just like real life! The other angle that these games can be approached from is the managerial one. You have to gain your team promotion from the Beazer Homes League right through to being World Club Champions via a combination of hire 'em fire 'em skills, cash "bungs" and even the occasional spot of honest wheeler dealing. You are the manager and like managers everywhere you can be sacked on the chairman's whim.

Adventures

If destroying everything in your path doesn't strike you as being the answer to the world's problems then an adventure game might suit. An adventure game is a massive verbal puzzle. At the start you are presented with a particular scenario in which the objective is explained to you. Actually achieving that objective involves hours of trial and error, mistake-making and lots and lots of lateral thinking. At its most primitive this type of game can be purely textual. A few sentences set the scene after which you are expected to enter your instructions "Inspect Object", "Go South", "Eat Cake", whatever. What happens next depends very much on what you have entered.

Early versions of these games were controlled purely by text input but most modern ones make full use of the Amiga's GUI. More advanced versions include graphics giving clues (not always helpful) and even allow you to control the movement of your character through the various scenes. At this stage the dividing line between this type of game and, say, a platform game can get quite blurred. A good adventure game will provide hours of mental stimulation with the most entertaining versions containing considerable wit in their creation.

Role Playing Games (RPGs) also belong in this category although they are often viewed through the eyes of a party of individuals a la Lord of the Rings. If you ever played Dungeons and Dragons or one its numerous clones then you'll appreciate the idea behind this game. Each individual member of the party has certain specific skills set at the start of the game and which can normally be enhanced as you go along. A whole team of players can play this game together.

Flight Sims

A flight simulation is as near as most of us will ever get to flying a real plane and, for the lucky few, one is often used as part of the training. The view you see on the screen is from the cockpit of your plane out onto a 3D modelled landscape. As you dip and dive around the landscape moves realistically around you, the effect is most impressive. The better the simulation the smoother the scene appears to scroll and the more features there will be dotted on the ground beneath you.

Once you have mastered the art of take-off, landing, stalling, crashing, and so on you need to have a competitive element to make it all the more exciting. This, predictably, comes in the form of an enemy of one type or another and it is your god-sworn duty to bomb, strafe and shoot them into oblivion. A well presented flight sim may only seem like a glorified shoot-em-up but the skill of trying to picture where an opponent is when you're manoeuvring in three dimensions calls for some amazing mental leaps. Your opponent in these dog-fights need not always be the computer. Some games let two joystick wagglers take to the air.

Puzzles

All your old favourites are to be found here – patience games, gambling games such as roulette or even fruit machines, picture puzzles with sliding blocks, computer versions of board games and so on.

Most of these are surprisingly simple in presentation and painfully addictive to use. *Tetris* and its numerous copies deserve a special mention. In this abstract game a series of coloured blocks descend from the top of the screen. As they descend you can rotate them and move them from left to right determining how they will eventually stack up at the bottom. You score different numbers of points for collections of for example yellow blocks and so on. It sounds incredibly dull described this way but should carry a health warning for its addictive qualities.

You might include in this category other cerebral challenges like Chess, Backgammon Othello, Scrabble, Trivial Pursuit and so on. As ever you can choose to play against a computer or a human opponent.

Strategy

War Games are an obvious candidate in this category. If you've ever spent hours with toy soldiers (and, presumably, considerable quantities of mud) re-enacting the Battle of the Somme then you'll be the first to appreciate how a computer can assume responsibility for the endless calculations required to measure the degrees of carnage you are reaping. Better than that it can also provide you with a graphical depiction of what is going on (fortunately not *that* graphical), maps of where you think your forces are deployed and where you suspect the enemy is and play out the drama in real time. In short, you can take on the role of General in any number of real or imaginary conflicts.

If the role of General is too humble then that of despotic dictator could be more up your street. In *Sim City* you are placed in control of a small but expanding village and you can add amenities as your budget permits. Village grows to town and town into city bringing with it the problems of urban decay, pollution, traffic congestion and even earthquakes or large monsters. If you've ever fancied trying your hand at a spot of town planning this is the game for you. The screen displays an aerial view of all that is happening in your city whilst providing you with all the tools you need to add a power station or a stretch of railway at just the click of a mouse button.

But if that still leaves your megalomanic cravings unsated then I suspect that nothing short of the role of God will satisfy. You can even do this in games like *Mega-lo-Mania* and the many versions of *Populous*. Your job is to nurture the development of a primitive tribe of people so that they become the dominant race on their own planet and can go and destroy any competing races. Yes, it does have an apocalyptic ring to it.

No round-up of types of games would be complete without mentioning *Lemmings*. I'm not sure whether this should be classified as a strategy game or a puzzle but it shows the levels of creativity that are being invested in computer games. The game presents you with a band of marauding lemmings all hell-bent on self-immolation. Your goal is to guide them through various hazards to some form of sanctuary without losing too many of the buggers on the way and without running out of time. This is done by clicking on individual lemmings and changing their otherwise suicidal behaviour. They can be made to dig holes, build bridges, block the movement of their compatriots, parachute safely down precipices or self-explode. If you've ever wondered what its like to be a teacher in charge of a classroom full of small, malevolent children then this is as near as you can get on a computer screen.

Game Over

These, then are the major types of games available though as I have said they don't have strict dividing lines between them. Which ones are the best? I'll leave that for you to find out – much depends on what you're looking for. The computer magazines are full of reviews of games and it is worth scanning the "budget" sections of these for the odd bargain or two.

Hints and Tips

The magazines don't just have comprehensive reviews of the latest games, they also supply details on how to get the most out of the latest favourite games that their readers (and staff) are playing. Most games are designed, whether intentionally or not, in such a way as to allow users to cheat their way past certain obstacles. The most common of these are the code words needed

Insider Guide #24: Running early games.

Games written explicitly for the A1200 have glorious colourful scrolling graphics that are a joy to behold but you are not restricted to using just these. Most of the games that were released for the other Amigas in the last two years before the arrival of the A1200 can run on the A1200. Of those that don't just a minor tweak to your machine might make them function.

Hold down the mouse buttons when you switch on the A1200 and you will find an "Amiga Early Startup Control" screen. In the middle of this are three buttons – click on the one marked "Display Options..." This brings up a separate screen which allows you to choose between various chip types. By default the "Best Available" option is highlighted but one or two games may work better in the "Enhanced" mode. Click on this option and then on the "Use" button and then try and boot up the game.

to get onto higher levels in the game. In normal play you are given a password each time you complete a level. The next time you play the game you can start at any level for which you have the password. It doesn't matter whether you found this out through honest toil or from the pages of a magazine. The magazines also provide anything from hints on strategy in the puzzle games to complete maps for adventure games and devious ways of gaining extra lives in shoot-em-ups. Let's face it, if you're stuck on a particular game then the odds are that someone else has been in a similar situation and has solved the problem...

Hardware

You need a joystick. Actually you don't need one at all but many games play much better with one. Apart from that the alternative is to use the buttons on your computer keyboard which is OK until you reach a particularly frantic part of the game when you'll find that you're giving the old qwerty one hell of a pounding.

As you can pick up a decent joystick for as little as a tenner it is going to be a worthwhile investment. True, you can pay a lot more than this but it does seem to be a law of diminishing returns.

Your purchasing needn't stop there. Some joysticks offer an autofire button which interrupts the signal sent to the computer. Thus by simply holding that button down the computer thinks you are hitting the fire button repeatedly. If you prefer the console approach where the joystick is replaced by a button pad you can attach one of those and, if that isn't enough, you can even buy foot pedals and steering wheels for racing car games.

**Most modern day computer languages have been
written specifically to make them easy to use.
That makes finding excuses for not programming
much harder to find...**

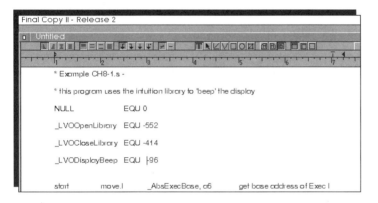

*C*omputer programming is the most fiendishly difficult process known to mankind. It is only ever done by strange men in white coats with round glasses and tufts of wild, grey hair or by socially inadequate teenagers who haven't seen the light of day – let alone another human being – in the years since they developed acne. In fact computer programming is nothing of the sort, it's just suffering problems in throwing off an unwelcome image.

Long Ago

The first time I ever tried programming a computer, each line of the program had to have its own sheet of cardboard which was about six inches by three inches in size. Each sheet had one program line printed across the top and a series of mysterious rectangular holes punched though on a grid beneath it. A great stack of these cards had to be handed over to the computer operator who told you to come back the following morning to collect your result. And, sure enough, the next morning there was your stack of cards with a small print-out attached saying on which line the program had failed. Great. For some reason computer programming never really appealed to me so I promise none of the following will involve punch-cards.

At about the same time as I was collecting punch-cards, flow charts were all the rage and no-one would seriously consider writing even the simplest program without drawing sheets and sheets of diagrams with diamonds, circles, rectangles, you name it all linked together by lines with arrows and cryptic "Yes" and "No" comments. Relax, we're not about to do any of that either.

It's true that time spent in advance, thinking through what you want a program to do, is time well spent but at this stage we're talking minutes not hours.

The first questions that a newcomer to this area should be asking are "What does computer programming entail?" and "Why would I want to bother?". That last question is particularly valid because you may decide after reading this chapter that it really isn't for you. And that's perfectly OK – it's eminently reasonable to use a computer on a daily basis, and for all manner of tasks, without ever deigning to program it.

Whatever you choose to do, though, it will improve your understanding of the whole process of computing if you have certain knowledge of the principles in operation.

"What does programming entail?" Well, just in case you are still convinced that programming is beyond your abilities it is worth remembering that AmigaDOS is a computer language. So, if you have been doing any of the AmigaDOS examples in this book, you have already been computer programming. AmigaDOS may not be the most suitable language to use for all your needs but it has many features common to the others. The most important of these being, at this stage, its ease of use.

Hard and Soft

The most important distinction to be made is that between hardware and software. The prefixes "hard" and "soft" don't always help because software has to be stored on some physical device that is, as you well know, hard. In principle, though, software is merely a set of instructions that tells the computer how to behave. The words software and programs are interchange-able.

Your A1200 will quite happily sit there all day until some software tells it what to do. Yes, the computer is just a glorified calculating machine. What is needed is the right set of calculations to get the most out of it. Software fills that role and software is written using computer lan-guages.

Engine Room

You are probably aware that, some-where deep within the mysterious workings of the machine all it is doing is a series of binary calculations involving streams of numbers that look like 101110, 1101, 1110011 and the like. It's all true but, to program a computer, you don't need to know how this works either. Sure, once you become a wizard at programming, you can get involved with this sort of thing but it's by no means obligatory.

Communicating with the computer in this manner is called "machine code programming". It involves sending instructions directly to the machine in a form that it can understand. After doing this for a while computer programmers realised that many of the commands they were writing they had used before. Rather than waste time repeating lengthy streams of code they began using a form of shorthand. A few letters could replace several hundred binary digits as long as, at some point before this was passed to the computer, these abbreviations were translated into binary code and the machine code assembled for the computer to understand. That was how the first computer languages were born. This sort of language, where the commands closely follow the way in which the machine thinks is called "low level" and is often called "Assembler".

As a low level language addresses the computer in a manner which it can easily understand, any programs written using it tend to be both small and fast. The other extreme is a "high level" language. Here the process of writing a program has been geared towards ease of use. A high level language's vocabulary contains words that are obvious in their meaning and use. AmigaDOS is one such language. "LIST" in AmigaDOS creates a list, COPY copies a file and DATE tells you the date. What more could you ask for? Between the two extremes are any number of languages that have various pros and cons.

Language Types

A command within a computer language is like a small machine code program. When you issue a command like "DATE" in AmigaDOS this is broadly speaking translated into machine code instructions that the A1200 understands.

So far we have thought of programs as being sets of instructions which the computer carries out one by one. Thus when it encounters a program, the computer assesses it line by line and carries out each line at a time. It translates each line into something that it can understand – this is called "interpreting".

In actual fact what actually happens is that the interpreter part of AmigaDOS first identifies the command by comparing it against an internal list of commands, and then extracts from this list the location of the start of the machine code responsible for actioning the command, which it then executes.

The alternative approach is for the computer to take the program in its entirety and translate it *en masse* into machine code. It is then ready to run in a form that the machine can understand. This process is called "compiling". Many languages will have either interpreted or compiled versions.

When writing a program in an interpreted language you can write a few lines, test it out, rewrite some lines, add a little more, test it out again, see what happens and so on until you reach a version you are happy with. To run an interpreted language requires that the interpreter is on hand to do its job.

When using a compiler you need to write the program, save it, run it through a compiler to produce something that the computer can understand, save that, and then run the end product. If that doesn't work then you have to go through the entire process all over again. The advantage of using a compiler is that the finished program is written in a form that the computer can directly understand. It doesn't have to bother interpreting anything on the way. As a consequence the program will run much faster.

Portability

AmigaDOS is an interpreted language. If you write an AmigaDOS script which uses the commands REQUESTCHOICE, LIST, DELETE, ASSIGN etc then the program won't run unless those commands are also available – normally they are in the C: directory on the SYS: disk. Should you wish, you could use an additional AmigaDOS command that you have written yourself. That would be fine as long as you also supplied that command to anyone else who wanted to use your program. Such a command might typically be written in machine code and could be made available separately to other AmigaDOS programmers if you thought it might be useful.

AmigaDOS was designed to take full advantage of the Amiga's powers. It cannot be run on any other computer and so it is called machine specific. Other languages like C and BASIC however, exist on pretty well any other computer you care to mention. A program written in one of these languages can, in theory, be written to run on any computer. The uncompiled version of a BASIC program written on a PC can be loaded into the compiler on an Amiga and should run quite happily. The stumbling blocks to this approach are that the program cannot contain any machine specific commands. If it does, it won't work on the new system.

While different computer languages can be used to write programs that do exactly the same sort of process, the manner in which they do it is usually completely different. A program written in C and a program written in BASIC might appear indistinguishable to the user but use fundamentally different approaches. So, for example, you can't just load a C program into a text editor, search and replace a few key words and then expect it to work as a BASIC program. Sorry.

Why Languages

When, for example, you wish to find the arithmetic mean (average) of three numbers it isn't important to you how the computer goes about doing it. What counts – if you'll pardon the pun – is that the computer takes the numbers you have supplied and comes back with the right answer. What you need is some means of saying to the computer:

"Find the average of A, B and C and tell me the answer"

The instructions to get the machine to do this could be written in all kinds of wierd and wonderful ways depending on the language you are using. For example, in one hypothetical language – let's call it "EZUU" – it might be a simple matter of saying that you want the mean found of the following numbers like so:

MEAN A,B,C

and the computer supplies the answer. "MEAN" is the command and "A", "B" and "C" its parameters.

The task appears to be beautifully simple but in reality the computer is doing an awful lot of your work for you.

But, in another language this might not be so simple. The instruction "MEAN" might not exist and you might have to go to great lengths explaining what you want doing. No prizes for guessing which language is going to be most popular for that sort of calculation. But what the two languages have in common is a vocabulary of words (like MEAN) which cause the computer to do a specific task.

The reason for this discrepancy is because different computer languages have been written for different purposes. Some have been designed with handling graphics as the foremost priority, others with calculating scientific equations. Happily some other languages have been written with the express purpose of being easy to use.

Command Syntax

When you think about it, the words of a computer language (its commands) are themselves like mini-programs. Each one instructs the computer to go through a series of lower-level processes. So the word of one computer language is a machine code program. It is possible, therefore, to write additional words to be used within a language – all they are is extra programs that you can make use of.

Just like a human language, computer languages have rules concerning their use. Unlike humans, computers aren't (yet!) capable of making sense of statements when the rules of grammar have been broken. Like a fusty scholar they insist on strict adherence to the rules of syntax. Use a particular word or command within a language incorrectly and an error will occur.

Same Routine

When you sit down to write your program you will usually find that some of the instructions that are needed, are needed over and over again. Rather than write them several times, give each routine a relevant title and save them for use on future occasions.

When someone else has written a routine to perform the task you want to achieve, don't go to all the trouble of trying to repeat the job yourself. Normally when you purchase a language a great library of routines comes with it to help you on your way. Not only that but you can buy more from PD libraries and the like, download them from bulletin boards or even find them on magazine disks.

Program Writing

Forget any notions you might have of drawing complex flowcharts or having to juggle with line numbers. They're all old hat.

However, it is always recommended that you sit down, away from the computer and plan out what it is that you want the program to achieve. Plan it in general terms and don't worry unduly about *how* you are going to program each step. What you should be able to do is to break up the program into manageable chunks. Having done this you may find that routines already exist for doing several of these chunks.

ARexx

ARexx (pronounced A-Rex) is the Amiga version of the REXX language to be found on other machines. Commodore have adopted it as part of Workbench 3.0. So to get started in ARexx programming all you need is a copy of your Workbench disks and some idea of what you're doing. The first part is easy the second is hardly any more taxing.

The files you need to use ARexx are on the Workbench disk and include: *System/RexxMast*
Libs:rexxsupport.library
Libs:rexxsyslib.library

and the *Rexxc* directory. If you are creating a cut-down version of the Workbench disk specifically for ARexx use then don't throw these files away.

ARexx programs can be written using any text processor that can produce an ASCII output. That means just about all of them and includes ED that you are already familiar with. For those of you who have programmed before in BASIC you will find many useful similarities between the programs which should help you get going although, conversely, you may need to un-learn certain things as well.

To get going in ARexx double-click on the RexxMast icon to be found in the System directory. This makes Rexx into a resident process which means that any ARexx scripts that you create and run will be interpreted into meaningful code.

Now open the Shell and type in the name of the ED file you wish to write your program in or use the "Execute Command..." option. For example:

ED RAM:EXAMPLE.REXX

This opens an ED window where you can write and save your program just like you would an AmigaDOS script. To run that program simply return to the Shell and type in:

RX EXAMPLE.REXX

This is about as far as I'm going to take you with ARexx, after all this isn't a programming manual. but there is plenty of high-quality documentation around should you need it.

AmigaDOS

We have already seen numerous examples of AmigaDOS at work both in script form and as a series of handy one-liners that can be entered in via the "Execute Command..." interface. As it is a fundamental part of the Workbench set-up you should be proficient in using at least some of its commands. As a programming language it is limited in its applications but for those processes it can be used for, it is usually the first choice.

AMOS

A BASIC-derived language, AMOS is particularly suitable for manipulating sound and graphics, hence its popularity with Amiga users. If you want to write games, then it is the language to use, but its uses are much greater than just that.

It comes in a variety of guises including Easy AMOS and the latest AMOS Professional which, I am assured, is especially good. There is also an AMOS Compiler so, once you have written your AMOS programs you can convert them into a much faster and more compact, machine code format. AMOS runs from its own editor screen. This

Insider Guide #25: Starting in ARexx.

Double-click on the RexxMast utility found in the System directory – this makes it a resident process.

Open the Shell and type in:

ED.RAM:GREET-INGS.REXX

In the ED window type in :

/* Greetings.rexx */

say 'What is your name?'

pull name

say 'Greetings 'name

and save the file (<Esc-X>). To run the ARexx program type in:

RX RAM:GREET-INGS.REXX

acts rather like a wordprocessor window, with a series of options along the top – such as "Load", "Save" and "Run".

All at C

C is a very popular high-level programming language which scores bonus points for its portability between operating systems. However, it has the ability to make low-level operations and as such is very flexible. For these reasons a lot of top notch serious software is written in C. It's a compiled language which does mean that you don't get the immediate response that you can with other languages but its other advantages far outweigh this.

Amiga BASIC

The most famous of computer languages is BASIC whose very name is an acronym for Beginners All-purpose Symbolic Instruction Code. You may already have come across versions of this language on other computers.

BASIC exists on the Amiga as well but it's getting a little long in the tooth these days and there are several other languages kicking around which are much easier to learn and much more powerful in what they can achieve – AMOS and ARexx.

Increasing the life expectancy of your A1200 is largely a matter of exercising some common sense...

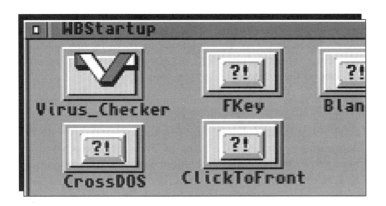

*I*t's easy to forget that the computer is quite a fragile piece of electronics. Looked after well it should last for years and years but things can go wrong. This chapter could be sub-titled "computing comon sense" as its main purpose is to explain why and how the more obvious precautions should be taken.

Floppy Disks

Floppy disks don't last for ever though some last longer than others. Try and keep a back-up copy of any valuable data in case the worst happens. When it does the disk won't be recognised by the A1200 when you put it in the disk drive. Instead the DF0:???? title will be displayed and the "Not a DOS disk" message will appear when you double-click on the icon. Depending on the damage done to the disk some of the data may be recoverable using the sort of utility designed just for this purpose – see *All is not Lost*.

Don't touch the surface of the disk and keep disks away from sources of heat and/or magnetism. So don't put them near your hi-fi or on top of the monitor.

Monitors

Avoid touching your monitor screen. As with most glass surfaces they tend to scratch too easily which creates all sorts of irritating reflections. Due to the static charge on the front of the screen, the monitor is a dust-trap. Clean it carefully with a proprietary screen-cleaning fluid and suitable cloth. Avoid "burn-in" of screen images – typically the Workbench screen – by using one of the innumerable screen blanking programs. BLANKER, which is one of the Commodities on the Extras disk, is more than adequate.

Monitors do tend to be very reliable and should last as long as your televsion set but if you're buying secondhand it's as well to remember that they don't last for ever. Tell-tale signs of old age include the intermittent disappearance of one of the three RGB colours. With a fully functioning monitor the red, green and blue colours are used in combination and in differing quantities to make up all other colours. White is produced by all three guns firing together. If the red gun isn't working the screen will appear turquoise, with the blue gun missing it will appear yellow and with the green gun missing it will appear pink. If a gun is missing it may be just a loose connection which your dealer will be able to fix. If it's the gun itself then the entire tube will need replacing which effectively means buying a new monitor.

Mice

As it gets rolled around the top of your work surface the mouse picks up tiny fragments of dust and fibres. Eventually these accumulate inside the mechanism clogging up the works. When this happens the mouse won't always respond to your movements and some rudimentary maintenance is called for.

Turn the mouse upside down and undo the catch to release the tracker ball. You will see, inside the mouse, the rollers that the ball moves against to control the pointer. You will probably also see tufts of fluff which should be pulled out. If the rollers themselves are dirty try using a cotton wool bud with a dab of white spirit to clean them. Using a mouse mat will reduce the amount of debris accumulated as well as giving better grip to the tracking ball.

Coffee & Smoke

It could be tea, beer, squash, a twelve year old malt or anything fluid but whatever it is, your Amiga doesn't like it as much as you do. The over-riding principle here is – don't. Don't bring them anywhere near your computer as the results can be both dangerous and expensive.

But if you do spill onto your computer then the first thing to do is switch off. Then try and minimise the damage by tipping the machine to drain away any surplus fluid.

Depending on how much you have spilt and where the situation may not be irretrievable. If it's a splash on the keyboard then you may be lucky. Take the machine to pieces, mop up any excess coffee that you find. Leave the rest to set into that familiar brown gunk and then try using a solvent-based cleaner to clear this out. You may be lucky.

If the spillage was further back on the machine then it's going to be an expensive trip to the dealers. Pouring coffee down the back of a monitor is one of the dumbest forms of entertainment going, so don't.

Tiny particles of smoke can settle on and cause damage to delicate surfaces everywhere: floppy disks, hard drives, lung tissue etc.

Hard Disks

Hard drives are expensive and should be treated with care. Apart from anything else there is the sheer inconvenience of having to start out from scratch. It isn't unusual for the hard disk to have a minor flaw somewhere on its surface and that isn't too much of a problem. If disk errors occur then hard disk can be reformatted but if it becomes commonplace then some sort of mechanical fault is likely and the unit should be replaced. Mechanical faults aren't in the habit of repairing themselves.

In normal use the surface of the hard drive's disks are spinning away fractions of an inch away from the heads that read them. If the two should come into contact you can expect to hear a high-pitched screeching noise. Hear that and you know it's curtains.

Guru Meditations

A black screen with orange writing on it in a flashing framed box. It's a guru meditation and something has gone wrong. If you haven't encountered one of these yet don't worry, you will. The good news is that the message is usually along the lines of "Recoverable alert. Press left mouse button to continue." Do so and you are returned to the Workbench window where all windows have been closed.

Software Crashes

A crash is about as bad as things get in normal computer use. The screen freezes and nothing you can do makes any difference. The computer doesn't respond to mouse or keyboard input. Nor does it respond to swearing or headbutting. The only option is to perform a soft-reboot which means losing all the work you have been working on.

Crashes are usually caused by badly written software trying to use one part of the processor to do two things at once or something equally *illegal* to use the programming jargon. In practice even the best software can suffer from these problems as it is nigh on impossible for programmers to prepare for every eventuality. The best precaution is to save data frequently. Some software even comes with an auto-save feature which updates the saved file every ten minutes or so.

Should one piece of software continually crash then contact the supplier making a note of any hardware add-ons you have and the circumstances when crashes occur. It may not be designed to cope with particular hardware combinations, alternatively your set-up may be infected with a virus.

Viruses

How do I know I've got one and what do I do about it? A lot has been written about viruses and the menace they pose but, with a little care, you should be able to avoid ever coming a cropper.

A virus is simply a program that has been deliberately written to cause heartache and headache to other computer users. They come in many different forms and, like real-life viruses, they can have a range of effects varying from the barely noticeable to the catastrophic. Viruses

Insider Guide #26: Avoiding the virus menace.

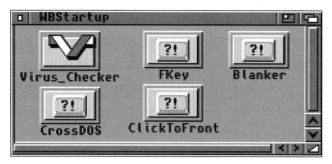

Place a virus killer inside the WBStartup file on your boot disk.

Each and every time you boot up the program is loaded. In normal use it will be invisible, working as a background task.

Try and get the most up-to-date version of any virus exterminator you can get hold of.

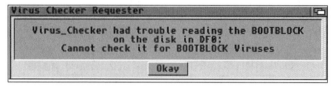

If you try to use a disk which has a dubious nature about it – a system request message will be displayed. Note that if you try to read a PC disk using CrossDOS – any installed virus checker will signal a potential problem when you insert the PC disk into the Amiga disk drive.

have been written that flash intermittent messages onto your screen, that redesign the pointer or other icons to something more obscene and that completely trash all your files. Some viruses lie dormant until a certain date and time is reached. In this respect a lack of internal clock on the A1200 looks like a definite plus.

How they Work

It is very easy to write a program to rename, copy or even delete files. To be a real computer virus the program has to be capable of making copies of itself and again that is pretty simple. The hardest part is getting such a program to run without the user being aware of what is happening. Once that has been achieved the virus can copy itself from disk to disk to hard drive to disk until such time as it starts making its presence felt. Obviously if the virus has some sort of delay element then it can quite feasibly have contaminated several disks before it is discovered.

Points to note:

- You can't locate viruses from within compressed files.

- Viruses don't survive the machine being switched off.

- They can't contaminate any disk that is write-protected.

- They aren't created spontaneously.

Virus Spotting

Some viruses make their presence blindingly obvious. This includes the obscene message or symbol variety or bizarre distortions of the screen picture. Others are more subtle and start shifting files around between directories. With one of these kinds of virus the first signs of trouble are often Workbench messages reporting the failure to load a program because a particular file has not been located. This second type is often much more difficult to locate because its effects can be caused by many, more mundane, reasons – operator error amongst them.

Take Precautions!

A virus-free life can't be guaranteed. You can take all the necessary precautions like installing a virus killer in your WBStartup directory, scan all incoming disks and never use disks from dubious sources and still end up being infected. How?

Well just as fast as virus killers are written to combat the threat, new viruses (or is it viri?) are being written to evade them. Should you encounter one of these viruses then your existing set up won't protect you. However, such an eventuality is unlikely. The writers of virus killing software often pride themselves on being bang up to date with all that's fashionable in computer infections. If you always have the latest software they have written then the chances on you stumbling across a new virus before they do is pretty slim. What you must do though is keep up to date on the latest versions of their software.

Although the majority of virus killers are freely copiable you should, if you are using that software, send a donation to the author. That way there is a strong incentive for the next version to be written.

Antibiotics

You need a piece of kit called a virus killer. Load this up from disk and depending on the severity of the virus you will be left with completely restored disks and software or with a mangled mess of files. If it's the latter then you can thank yourself for having been prudent enough to make copies of all your most important files...

Close Down

At the end of the day, when you've finished using your computer, don't forget to switch it off. Before you do, though, wait for a few seconds. If you are in the process of saving a file before switch-off then give this time to be completed. The computer often gives the impression of having finished saving while there is still data saving taking place. Switching off while this goes on is one of the easiest ways to corrupt your files.

Don't switch the A1200 back on immediately after switching it off. There are two reasons for this:

- The electronic components still bear some capacitance after shutdown. Switching back on before this has fully dissipated can overload them causing failure. Leave thirty seconds between switching off and switching back on and you should have no trouble at all.

- Hard disks, if fitted, continue to spin for a short while after shutdown. Restarting the machine can cause data corruption. The thirty second wait should, again, be more than sufficient for their protection.

And that's it. With a little bit of care your A1200 should provide you with many trouble-free years of computing. I hope it goes well...

The Next Steps Disk of freely distributable
software to accompany the chapters in this book
is available from Bruce Smith Books.

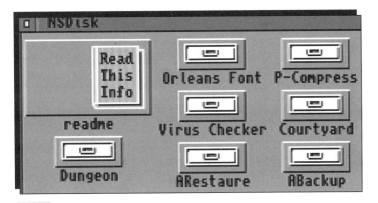

*T*he *Next Steps Disk* contains those utilities that are most
frequently needed to speed up the whole process of computing on your A1200. To use the disk insert it into your
A1200 drive and double-click on the *Next Steps Disk* icon when
it appears. This will display a window which will reveal several
icons. Double-click on the ReadMe icon for more up-to-date
information relating to the book.

ARestaure   File recovery utility. Rescues files that have
                    been deleted

ABackup   Makes up-to-date copies of data for protec-
                    tion. Ideal for backing up a hard drive.

Virus Checker   Protect against infection. Save your programs
                    from attack.

P-Compress   Reduces file sizes to save space

Orleans   Outline font – improve your presentation and
                    create additional bitmap fonts.

SoundFX   Sound Effect files – to customise your Workbench or add to soundtracker files.

Dungeon   MultiView file – as shown in MultiView chapter

ReadMe   File listing any changes to this book since publication.

Courtyard   Picture as used in the PrintOut chapter. Compare your own results with ours.

Send a cheque/PO for £1.50 made payable to Bruce Smith Books Ltd to:

Next Steps Disk
Bruce Smith Books
PO Box 382,
St Albans,
Herts AL2 3JD.

Orders originating from the USA or Australia should send a $5 bill to cover all costs.

We've taken you through the doorway of your Amiga A1200 – now open it wide to the extensive range of Insider Guides and Mastering Amiga titles available from the world's number one Amiga Book publisher – Bruce Smith Books.

*B*ruce Smith Books is dedicated to producing quality Amiga publications which are both comprehensive and easy to read. Our Amiga titles are written by some of the best known names in the marvellous world of Amiga computing. If you have found that your *Insider Guide* has proved informative and want to delve deeper into your Amiga then why not try one of our highly rated *Mastering Amiga* guides? In other words – if you enjoyed getting insider your Amiga, now is the time to master it!

Below you will find details of all our books in the *Mastering Amiga* and *Insider Guide* range that are either currently available or due for publication soon.

Compatibility

We endeavour to ensure that all Mastering Amiga books are fully compatible with all Amiga models and all releases of AmigaDOS and Workbench. The Mastering AmigaDOS books are constantly updated to reflect Commodore's evolving Amiga operating system so you can be sure that these bibles of Amiga computing will keep up to date with you and your computer. Please check the list of titles currently and soon to be available below for full compatibility with your particular machine.

Book	A500	A500+	A600	A1200	A2000	A3000	A4000
Mastering AmigaDOS2 Vol. 1	Y	Y	Y‡	N	Y	Y*	N
Mastering AmigaDOS2 Vol. 2	Y	Y	Y‡	N	Y	Y*	N
Mastering AmigaDOS3 Vol. 1	N	N	N	Y	N	Y#	Y
Mastering AmigaDOS3 Vol. 2	N	N	N	Y	N	Y#	Y
Mastering Amiga Workbench2	N	Y	Y	N	Y	Y*	N
Mastering Amiga Beginners	Y†	Y	Y	Y	Y†	Y	Y
Amiga Gamer's Guide	Y	Y	Y	Y	Y	Y	Y
Mastering Amiga AMOS	Y	Y	Y	Y	Y	Y	Y
Mastering Amiga C	Y	Y	Y	Y	Y	Y	Y
Mastering Amiga Printers	Y	Y	Y	Y	Y	Y	Y
Mastering Amiga System	Y	Y	Y	Y	Y	Y	Y
Mastering Amiga Assembler	Y	Y	Y	Y	Y	Y	Y
Mastering Amiga ARexx	N	Y	Y	Y	Y	Y	Y
Amiga A600 Insider Guide	N	N	Y	N	N	N	N
Amiga A1200 Insider Guide	N	N	N	Y	N	N	N
Amiga A1200 Next Steps	N	N	N	Y	N	N	N
Workbench 3 A-Z Insider Guide	N	N	N	Y	N	Y#	Y
Amiga Assembler Insider Guide	N	N	Y	Y	Y	Y	Y

Y† State if you have AmigaDOS 1.3   Y* Earlier versions with AmigaDOS2
Y‡ 80% compatible with 2.1 version   Y# Latest versions with AmigaDOS3

Brief details of these guides along with review segments are given below. If you would like a free copy of our catalogue and to be placed on our mailing list then phone or write to the address below.

You can order a book simply by writing or using the simple tear our form to be found towards the end of this book.

Our mailing list is used exclusively to inform readers of forthcoming Bruce Smith Books publications along with special introductory offers which normally take the form of a free software disk when ordering the publication direct from us.

Bruce Smith Books, PO Box 382, St. Albans, Herts, AL2 3JD
Telephone: (0923) 894355 – Fax: (0923) 894366

Note that we offer a 24-hour telephone answer system so that you can place your order direct by 'phone at a time to suit yourself. When ordering by 'phone please:

- Speak clearly and slowly
- Leave your full name and full address
- Leave a day-time contact phone number
- Give your credit card number and expiry date
- Spell out any unusual names

Note that we do not charge for P&P in the UK and we endeavour to dispatch all books within 24-hours.

Buying at your Bookshop

All our books can be obtained via your local bookshops – this includes WH Smiths which will be keeping a stock of some of our titles – just enquire at their counter. If you wish to order via your local High Street bookshop you will need to supply the book name, author, publisher, price and ISBN number – these are all summarised at the very end of this appendix.

Overseas Orders

Note that our books are available direct from your local dealer in the following countries: USA, Australia, New Zealand, Scandinavia, and Benelux. If your local dealer does not have details please contact us direct for the name of your distributor.

Otherwise, please add £3 per book (Europe) or £6 per book (outside Europe) to cover postage and packing. Pay by sterling cheque or by Access, Visa or Mastercard. Post, Fax or Phone your order to us.

Dealer Enquiries

Our distributor is Computer Bookshops Ltd who keep a good stock of all our titles. Call their Customer Services Department for best terms on 021-706-1188.

Summary Book Details

Amiga A600 Insider Guide by Bruce Smith

ISBN: 1-873308-14-0, price £14.95, 256 pages.

A perfect companion for all A600 and A600HD users. This book provides you with a unique insight into the use of Workbench and AmigaDOS on all versions of the Amiga A600.

Assuming no prior knowledge it shows you how to get the very best from your machine in a friendly manner and using its unique Insider Guide steps (see A1200 description below).

Amiga A1200 Insider Guide by Bruce Smith

ISBN: 1-873308-15-9, price £14.95, 256 pages.

The world's best selling A1200 book! Assuming no prior knowledge, it shows you how to get the very best from your A1200 in a friendly manner and using its unique Insider Guide steps. Configuring your system for printer, keyboard, Workbench colours, use of Commodities and much much more has made this the best-selling book for the A1200.

As well as easy to read explanations of how to get to grips with the Amiga, the book features 55 of the unique Insider Guides, each of which displays graphically a set of step by step instructions. Each Insider Guide concentrates on a especially important or common task which the user has to carry out on the Amiga. By following an Insider Guide the user learns how to control the Amiga by example. Beginners to the A1200 will particularly appreciate this approach to a complex computer.

The disks which come with the A1200 contain a wealth of utilities and resources which allow you to configure the computer for your own way of working. The step by step tutorials take you through using these point by point, anticipating any problems as they go. There are also fully fledged programs such as MultiView and ED which can seem impenetrable for the new user but which become clear when observed in use over the shoulder of author Bruce Smith.

Great new features such as the colour wheel, Intellifonts, using MSDOS disks with CrossDos and configuring sound are dealt with in detail. A useful appendix acts as a file locater so that any of the many files on the Amiga disks can be quickly found.

Workbench 3 A to Z Insider Guide by Bruce Smith

ISBN: 1-873308-28-0, Price £14.95, pages TBA. Available Dec. 93.

From the world's number 1 selling Amiga book author comes this indispensible guide to Workbench 3 which covers every aspect of the Amiga Workbench version 3. Complete, with illustrations it provides comprehensive coverage of every Workbench menu option and icon across every disk – and more.

An indispensible guide and essential reference for every Workbench 3 owner!

Assembler Insider Guide by Paul Overaa

ISBN: 1-873308-27-2, Price £14.95, 256 pages. Available Nov. 93.

The Amiga Assembler Insider Guide has been written for the new user who wishes to learn to write programs in the native code of the Amiga computer – assembly language.

The approach taken to this, often daunting, subject is designed to achieve practical results. This is done through short examples which demonstrate different programming skills. Each program in the book can be assembled and run in under one minute so the beginner need have no fear of long impenetrable listings. This is programming for the novice, made all the easier though the mini Insider Guides which summarise important operations and fundamental concepts.

The author Paul Overaa writes many articles on programming and runs columns for beginners to programming so his style is carefully crafted for the programming newcomer. Possible stumbling blocks and areas which regularly cause beginners problems are taken head on. The issue of using Commodore libraries, and not using them is dealt with. No extra software is required to run the examples provided. After reading the book, the user will be able to confidently type in and edit source code, assemble it, debug it and and run it.

The book is compatible with all the main assemblers on the market. A support disk is available from the publisher which contains the A68K assembler, all the listings in the book, additional utilities and examples (cost £2.00 P&P). With the Amiga Assembler Insider Guide learning assembler on the Amiga has never been easier.

Mastering Amiga Beginners by Bruce Smith and Mark Webb

ISBN: 1-873308-17-5, Price £19.95, 320 pages.

Mastering Amiga Beginners is the book for the growing number of novice computer users who turn to the Amiga as the natural computer for home entertainment and self-education.

The authors have built up a wide experience of beginners' requirements and the problems they encounter and now this vast knowledge of the subject has been distilled into 320 pages of sensible advice and exciting ideas for using the Amiga.

Mastering AmigaDOS 3 Tutorial by Smith and Smiddy

ISBN: 1-873308-20-5, Price £21.95, 416 pages approx. Avail. Nov. 93. FREE disk with all the scripts and programs from the book when ordered direct.

The beginners part of the Mastering AmigaDOS3 dual volume set is a complete tutorial to AmigaDOS, designed to help the beginner become the expert. From formatting a disk to multi-user operation, over 400 pages spans every aspect of the Amiga's operation. The book is packed with DOS one-liners and scripts.

Mastering AmigaDOS 3 A to Z Reference by Mark Smiddy

ISBN: 1-873308-18-3 Price £21.95 416 pages.

The complete A to Z reference to DOS commands for A1200 and 4000 owners. The action of each command is explained and examples to try are provided. Chapters on AmigaDOS error codes, viruses, the Interchange File Format (IFF) and the Mountlist complete this valuable guide.

Mastering AmigaDOS 2 Volume One – Revised Edition by Bruce Smith and Mark Smiddy

ISBN: 1-873308-10-8 Price £21.95 416 pages. FREE disk with all the scripts and programs from the book.

The beginners AmigaDOS book for A500, A500 Plus, A2000 and A600 owners.

Mastering AmigaDOS 2 Volume Two – Revised Edition by Bruce Smith and Mark Smiddy

ISBN: 1-873308-09-4 Price £19.95 368 pages.

The A to Z AmigaDOS reference book for A500, A500 Plus, A2000 and A600 owners.

Mastering Amiga C by Paul Overaa
ISBN: 1-873308-04-6 Price £19.95 320 pages. FREE Programs Disk and NorthC Public Domain compiler when ordered direct.

Learn C for fun or profit with this easy to use guide to the language which is the natural language for Amiga programming. Ideal for anyone using their Amiga to catch up on computer studies!

Mastering Amiga Printers by Robin Burton
ISBN: 1-873308-05-1 Price £19.95 336 pages. FREE Programs disk when ordered direct.

After reading Mastering Amiga Printers, any Amiga owner will be able to choose effectively the ideal printer for his or her requirements. The Amiga's own printer control software is pulled apart and explained from all points of view, from the Workbench to the operating system routines. Individual printer drivers are assessed and screen-dumping techniques explained.

Mastering Amiga System by Paul Overaa
ISBN: 1-873308-06-X Price £29.95 398 pages. FREE disk when ordered direct.

Serious Amiga programmers need to use the Amiga's operating system to write legal, portable and efficient programs. But it's not easy! Paul Overaa shares his experience in this introduction to system programming in the C language. The author keeps it specific and presents skeleton programs which are fully documented so that they can be followed by the newcomer to Amiga programming. The larger programs are fully-fledged examples which can serve as templates for the reader's own ideas as confidence is gained.

Mastering Amiga Assembler by Paul Overaa
ISBN: 1-873308-11-6 Price £24.95 416 pages. FREE disk when ordered direct.

This book explains the use of assembly language to write efficient code within the unique environment of the Amiga, doing so without duplicating standard 68000 material. Instruction is achieved by short code examples amidst discussion of the issues involved in using machine code for various purposes. Subjects covered in over 400 pages include cooperation with the System software, custom chips and the C language. All the popular Amiga assemblers are supported by the many code examples in this book.

Mastering Amiga AMOS by Phil South

ISBN: 1-873308-13-2 Price £19.95 320 pages.

Ideal for anyone investing in AMOS, EasyAMOS or AMOS Professional. Full of hints, tips and shortcuts to effective and spectacular AMOS programming, the book also contains many useful routines and program design ideas.

Mastering Amiga ARexx by Paul Overaa

ISBN: 1-873308-13-2 Price £21.95 336 pages. FREE disk with all the ARexx examples and utilities when ordered direct.

Now a standard part of Commodore's software strategy, ARexx has been much admired by the programming community and is now available to all. This book is an ideal companion to the ARexx documentation, explaining the important concepts and providing a hands-on introduction to programming.

Amiga Gamer's Guide by Dan Slingsby

ISBN: 1-873308-16-7 Price £14.95 368 pages.

From sports sims to arcade adventures, Amiga Gamer's Guide gives you the hints and tips, hidden screens and puzzle solutions which you are looking for. Completed by a massive A to Z of tips and tricks for over 300 games, Amiga Gamer's Guide is the most masterful of games guides yet published.

Written by *CU Amiga* editor Dan Slingsby, Amiga Gamer's Guide contains a wealth of background information to the most popular Amiga games. The graphically appealing layout with hundreds of pictures used to illustrate the games and their storylines, makes this one of the most attactive Amiga books to be found on the bookshelves.

NOTE

Note: Disks where indicated are supplied free only when ordered direct from Bruce Smith Books. Otherwise disk are available from BSB for a nominal charge.

E&OE.

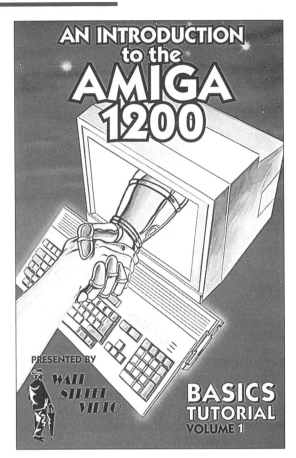

NEW from Bruce Smith Books in association with Wall Street Video –
Australia's leading Amiga training company – the perfect video introduction to using your Amiga A1200 and a perfect companion for the
world's top selling A1200 book, Bruce Smith's classic *Amiga A1200
Insider Guide.* This one hour video provides a basic tutorial on how to
set up and run your Amiga A1200 by using great animations and split
screens to increase your understanding of the concepts being explained.
Re-examine those tricky *grey areas* by instantly rewinding the video!

Applicable to both hard and floppy disk users the *Amiga A1200 Video*
may also be used to understand the Amiga A4000 and at £14.99 represents outstanding value. Available from all good stores or direct from
BSB. Simply phone (0923) 894355 to place your credit card order,
today!

Index

8SVX 56, 57, 204
<Ctrl><Amiga><Amiga> 68, 122
<Ctrl><C> 91, 92
>NIL: 99

A

A2024 ....150, 153
Abort..91
About..19
acceleration...33
accelerator 139, 140
access speed..160
ADDBUFFERS...98, 114
AGA 149, 150
ALIAS 50, 51, 107
ALL...46
AmigaDOS 43, 105, 117, 216, 217, 219, 222
AmigaDOS flags..78, 83
AmigaGuide 56, 57, 58
AMOS...222, 224
animation...192, 195
Apple Macintosh...144
archive flag 83
archiving 83, 90
ARexx 221, 223, 224
ASCII.............................36, 39, 105, 144, 145, 147
asl.library..104
aspect ratio 78, 129, 130
assembler..217
ASSIGN...51, 99, 175
Atari ST...145
AudioIFF 204
AutoPoint...39, 40
Autoscroll...155

B

back-up 46, 88, 174, 176, 177, 178, 181
Backdrop..18
BASIC..219, 221, 222, 224
baud rate 139
beat-em-ups 209
binary 217
BINDDRIVERS 100, 102

bitmap 74, 75, 78, 79
Blanker 38, 39, 226
bold 74
boot disk ....
.........97, 99, 101, 102, 104, 172
break 91, 92
buffer 98, 114
bug...........................98, 128
bulletin boards 139
bytes 78

C

C 219, 224
Calculator 36, 108
camcorder 144, 194
Caps Lock 39
CD 47, 107
CD-ROMS 142
CD32 143
change main device 36, 134, 135
chaos 192
Classes 99
Clean Up 21
CLEAR 51
ClickToFront 39, 40
Clipboards 99
CLIPS: 99
CLONE 167
Close 21
CMD 36, 134, 135
co-processor 140
codes 144
comma separated variable ...145
Commodities 38
commodities.library............104
Commodities Exchange 38
compiler 218
compressed files 230
compression 89, 177
computer paper..................126

ConClip 101
condensed fonts 74
condition testing 111, 112
COPY ...24, 46, 67, 99, 123, 167
crash.....................68, 176, 228
CrossDOS 39, 40, 147
crosswires 57
CSV 145
current directory..................46
current window 20
cylinder 92

D

daisywheel printer 125
data types 56
database 59, 139
DataTypes...........................56
DATE 51, 118, 119
DBLNTSC 153
DBLPAL 153
decompression 89, 177
Default Tool 172
default 97
DELETE 44, 46, 87, 91, 120
delete flag 83
Delete... 25
deleting files 91, 92, 93
delta animation..................196
density 129, 131
DESTINATION disk 91
desktop publishing 74, 139, 144
device................................68
DEVS: 100
digitising 144, 193
DIR.................................44
directories 17, 78
Directory Cache 25, 26
directory tree 56
disk drives 138

DISKCOPY ....
......46, 47, 67, 70, 91, 123, 124
DISKFONT 78
display modes 151, 152, 155
dithering 129, 130
dot-matrix printer 125, 126
dot-pitch 150
double-click 33
download 139
draggable 158
DRAM......................188, 189
drawers 17
drop capitals 76
DTP 74, 139, 144
dual sync 150, 197
Dynamic RAM 188

E

ECHO 50, 51
ECS 158
ED 48, 59, 78, 105
ED commands 83
EEPROM 188
elephants............................188
ELSE 111
Empty Trash 26
emulator 146
ENDCLI 51, 101
ENDIF 99
ENDSHELL 51
enhanced chip set...............158
ENV 99
ENV/Sys 99
environmental variable ...78, 99
Epson-compatible 127
erased files.....................91, 92
EURO:36Hz 153
EURO:72Hz 154
Exchange 38
EXECUTE 49, 99
Execute Command... 18, 118-124

EXISTS 99, 100, 101
Expansion 100
Extras disk 29, 76, 167

F

facsimile 142
FAILAT 98
failed 104
fancy fonts 76
Fast File System............25, 139
fax.................................142
file header 59, 89
file rescue 95
file translator.....................145
file type 56, 59
FILENOTE.........................120
Filenotes 24
FKey 39, 40
flags 78, 81, 83
flicker 155, 157
flight simulations 210
floating point unit 140
floppy disk drive 67
Fonts 32, 74-76, 99
Fonts disk 76, 167
FORCE 120
FORMAT 48, 91, 108
Format Disk...............25, 26, 91
FPU 140
fractal generator 192
FTXT 56, 57
function key 39, 41

G

games 97, 173, 207
Generic 127, 132
genlock 194
GIF 145
global environmental
                    variables......99
Gothic 74

Graphic Dump......................36
Graphical User Interface 30
graphics cards 157, 197
grey scales 129, 130
GUI...................................30
guru meditations 228

H
hard disk drive.........................
......67, 139, 159, 171, 227, 231
hardware add-ons 38
HDToolBox 160, 166
header...........................59, 89
Help 76
HELP: 99
Helvetica 74
Hewlett-Packard 127
hieroglyphics 74
High Res 153, 154
high density disk drives 138
high resolution 78
high-level language 217
HighCyl 70
hot-keys 26, 27, 28
hypertext 57

I
IBM PCs 144
Icon Text 33
icon names 78
IconEdit 36
Icons Menu 22
icons 17
IControl 155
IDE 160, 166
IF 99, 111
IF... ELSE... 111
IFF ....
31, 32, 57, 63, 145, 200, 201, 204
ILBM 56, 57, 145
image processing 144

INFO 122
Information 24, 40, 86, 172
Initprinter...........................36
inkjet printer 125
Input 33
INSTALL 102, 113, 114, 124
installing software 175
Intellifont 30, 76-78
interlaced 153, 154, 156
International Mode 25
interpreter 218
IPrefs 101

J
JOIN...............................108

K
keyboard 33
keymaps 33
KEYMAPS: 99
Keyshow 36
Kickstart 3.1 143
Kickstart 18, 19, 100, 143

L
laced 153, 154, 156
Lacer 36
laser printer 125
Last Message 19
launch 124
Leave Out 24
LEDs 163
LIBS: 99
LIST 22, 45, 78, 119, 121
LoadWB 101
Locale....................34, 58, 167
LOCALE: 99
LOCK 121
looping 196
Low Res 153, 154

low-level language 217
Lucida 74

M
machine code.....................217
Make Sound 31
MAKEDIR...............45, 46, 122
Mandlebrot........................192
margins 132
masking 195
maths co-processor 140, 184
MEmacs 36, 108
Micro-EMACS...............36, 108
MIDI 202
Mode Properties 155, 158
modem 139
modifier............................44
Monitors 100, 150, 226
MORE 105, 115, 116, 118
morphing 192
MOUNT 100, 114
mountfile 69
mountlist 70
mouse 226
mouse speed........................33
MouseBlanker 39, 40
MS-DOS 39, 40
multi-tasking 123
multiple copies 70
MULTISCAN 154
multisync 150, 157, 197
MULTIVIEW 61, 124
MultiView 55, 105, 124

N
network 139
New Drawer 20
NEWCLI 51
NEWSHELL.........................51
No PopUp 40
NoCapsLock 39, 40

node 59
NONUM 110
NTSC 152, 154, 192

O
On Line 126
on-line help 76
Open 22
Open Parent 21
optical disks 177
outline fonts 75, 76
Overscan 34
overwrite 92

P
pages 57
PAL 78, 152, 154, 192
PAL encoder 198
Palette 34, 156
Paper Feed 126
Parallel 128
Parent 56
parking 176
partition 166, 167, 177, 179
PATH...........................51, 101
pattern matching 46
PC 144, 145, 146
PCD 107
PCMCIA...38, 178, 185, 186, 189
platform games 208
point size 74, 78
Pointer 35
pointer 33
Preference Editors 30
Preference settings 101
Preferences ....
...............29, 30, 32, 127, 128,
...........................132, 150, 156
Prefs drawer........................30
PrepCard 38, 189
Printer 35

printer driver 127, 133
PrinterGFX 35, 129, 130
PRINTERS: 99
PRINTFILES 36, 134
printhead 126
printing 125
printing to a file 133, 134
Process 123
processor 139
productivity 155
programming 48, 215
PROMPT 52
PROTECT 83, 88
pure flag 84
Put Away 25

Q

Quick Format 26, 96
QUIET 98
Quit...................................20

R

RAD disk 67, 69, 71, 77, 100,
..........................114, 139, 169
RAM 114, 137, 183
RAM upgrade 38
Ram Disk 67, 93, 95, 99
raw 144
ray-tracing..................139, 192
read 78
ReadMe files 115, 116
reboot 68, 70
Redraw All 18
RELABEL...........................47
removable hard drive 177
REMRAD 70, 115
RENAME 48
Rename... 24
REQUESTCHOICE 112, 113
reset....................................68, 70
ResetWB 26

RESIDENT 52, 99, 108
Restore to Defaults 35
Retrace 57
REXX 99, 221
RGB 150, 192
role-playing games 210
ROM.....................97, 142, 143
routines 220
RPGs 210
RUN..............................44, 50

S

Sampled Sound 31
sampling 200, 204
San Serif.......................74, 76
scaling 129
scanners 144
SCREEN 61, 124
screen drag.......................155
screen mode61, 78, 156, 193, 194
screen refresh rate 195
ScreenMode 35, 151
script 48
script flag 84
SCSI 160, 166, 184
SEARCH 109
Select Contents 21
sequencer 203, 203
Serial 35
Serif...............................74, 76
SETENV 100
SETPATCH 98
Shell 44, 51, 78, 105, 117
shoot-em-ups.....................208
Show 20
Show >> All Files 20
Show >> Only Icons 20
ShowConfig 38
smart cards 186
smoothing 129
SMPTE 197

Snapshot 21, 22, 24
soft reboot 68, 70
soft-boot 68, 70
SORT 110
Sound 31
SOURCE disk 91
speed 139
sports simulations 209
spreadsheet 139
SRAM 186, 188
startup 97
Startup-Sequence ....
....................97, 102, 106, 114
Static RAM 186, 188
STATUS 123
Storage 33, 68, 127
Storage disk 167
STRING 109
subroutines 220
SUPER72 154
SYS:Fonts 99
System 43

TYPE 53, 105, 118
type....................................74
typeface 74

U
unknown command 104
UNSET 101
Unsnapshot 24
Update..........................21, 23
Update All..........................18
User-Startup 101, 175

V
VCR..........................192, 193
VERSION 18, 38, 53, 98
VGA 100
video recorder 192, 193
video titling 78, 194
video toaster 197
View By 20
virus 174, 228, 229

T
T 99
temporary files 99
Text 33
threshold 129, 131
TIFF................................145
Time 35
Times................................76
toggle................................25
Tool Menu 26
Tool Types 24, 40
Tools 29, 36
Tracker 145
Trackers 201
tractor feeding 126
translations 56, 145
trapdoor....................184, 186
Trashcan 25, 167

W
WBPattern 35, 36
WBStartup 230
wildcards 53
WIMP................................17
Window menus 20
wordprocessor 73, 74, 78
wordwrap 59
Workbench 3.1 143
Workbench ....
............17, 29, 78, 100, 143, 167
Workbench disk 76
Workbench Icon Text 33
Workbench menus 18
write 78
write-protection ....
..................78, 81, 84, 189, 230
WYSIWYG 74

"The Mastering Amiga series provides top quality guidance for Amiga users."

...but don't just take our word for it!

"If you're a beginner or a newcomer to Amigas, these two books provide an excellent way of finding your way around your new machine"

Richard Baguley, Amiga Format on the
A600 and A1200 Insider Guide series.
AF GOLD AWARD – 90%

"This book has been written with the absolute novice in mind. It doesn't patronise, yet neither does it baffle with jargon and slang"

Chris Lee, CU Amiga Review on Mastering Amiga C.

"I have to say that the best hands-on tutorial that I've seen is Mastering AmigaDOS 2 Volume One."

Pat McDonald, Amiga Format on Mastering AmigaDOS Vol. 1.

"The definitive book on the subject, don't leave your Workbench without it!"

Neil Jackson, Amiga Format on Mastering AmigaDOS Vol. 2.

"...it's well worth buying a decent book on the subject – I personally recommend you get Mastering Amiga Printers."

Jason Holborn, Amiga Format on Mastering Amiga Printers.

"The latest in the excellent range of specialist Amiga Books... covers every aspect of the complex Amiga system"

Damien Noonan, Amiga Format on Mastering Amiga System.